LETTER

ON THE TRUTHS

CONTAINED

IN POPULAR SUPERSTITIONS

BY

HERBERT MAYO M. D.

PUBLISHED BY
JOHN DAVID SAUERLÆNDER, FRANKFORT O/M.
AND
MESS^{RS} BLACKWOOD, EDINBURGH.
1849.

Kessinger Publishing's Rare Reprints
Thousands of Scarce and Hard-to-Find Books!

We kindly invite you to view our extensive catalog list at:
http://www.kessinger.net

PREFATORY REMARKS

The original letters appeared in Blackwood's magazine in 1847. The superstitions examined are, the divining rod, vampyrism, the belief in ghosts and dreams, second-sight, supposed workings of the holy spirit on masses, possession by devils (in the middle ages and subsequently), witchcraft. The truths expounded are, the Od force, the law of sensorial illusions, the laws of trance. The superstitions reduced to natural phenomena fall thus into the domain of physiology, and their elucidation enriches one of its most important sections. In revising the letters for republication, I have been led to recast them, and have to a considerable extent rewritten the theoretical part. I have likewise added some striking facts to the body of instances before adduced. These facts and instances are I think sufficiently strange and curious to interest the idlest reader; — for whose convenience, and my own pleasure, I have compressed the appended philosophy into a nutshell, fit emblem possiply of its value. It grew in the slow progress of my thoughts as the necessary complement to my views on "the nervous system and its functions," matured, and published under that title before I left England in 1842, by Messrs. Parker. They too lie in small compass. What one sees clearly one can express briefly. What admits of being the most clearly seen is truth.

January 1. 1849.
BOPPARD ON THE RHINE.

ON THE TRUTHS
CONTAINED
IN POPULAR SUPERSTITIONS

Letter I
THE DIVINING ROD

Dear Archy,

As a resource in the solitary evenings of commencing winter it occurred to me to look into the long-neglected lore, of the marvellous, the mystical, the supernatural. I remembered the deep awe with which I had listened many a year ago to tales of seers, ghosts, vampyrs, and all the dark brood of night. And I thought it would be infinitely agreeable to thrill again with mysterious terrors, to start in my chair at the closing of a distant door, to raise my eyes with uneasy apprehension towards the mirror opposite, and to feel my skin creep through the sensible "afflatus" of an invisible presence. I entered accordingly upon a very promising course of appalling reading. But, alack and well-a-day, a change had come over me since the good old times, when fancy, with fear and superstition behind her, would creep on tiptoe to catch a shuddering glimpse of kobbold, Fay, or Incubus. Vain were all my efforts to revive the pleasant horrors of earlier years. It was as if I had planned going to a play to enjoy again the full gusto of scenic illusion, and through absence of mind was attending a morning rehearsal only; when instead of what I had anticipated, great coats, hats, umbrellas, and ordinary men and women, masks, tinsel, trap-doors, pulleys, and a world of intricate machinery, lit by a partial gleam of sunshine, had met my view. The enchantment was no longer there; the spell was broken.

Yet on second thoughts the daylight-scene was worth contemplating. A new object of stronger interest suggested itself. I might examine and learn the mechanism of the illusions which had failed to furnish me the projected entertainment. In the books I had looked into, I discerned a clue to the explanation of many wonderful stories, which I could hitherto only seriously meet by disbelief. I saw that phenomena, which before had appeared isolated, depended upon a common principle itself allied with a variety of other singular facts and observations, which wanted only to be placed in philosophical juxta-position to be recognized as belonging to science. So I determined to employ the leisure before me upon an inquiry into the amount of truth in popular superstitions; certain, that if the attempt were not premature, the labour would be well repaid. There must be a real foundation for the belief of ages. There can be no prevalent delusion without a corresponding truth. The visionary promises of alchemy fore-shadowed the solid performances of modern chemistry; — as the debased worship of the Aegyptians implied the existence of a proper object of worship.

Among the immortal productions of the Scottish Shakespeare, you smile, but that phrase contains the true belief not a popular delusion; for the spirit of the poet lives not in the form of his works, but in his creative power and vivid intuitions of nature; and the form even is often nearer than you think; but this discursiveness will never do; to begin again,

Among the novels of Scott, — I intended to say, there is not one more wins upon us than the Antiquary. Nowhere has the great author more gently and indulgently, never with happier humour described the mixed web of strength and infirmity in human character; never besides with more facile power evoked pathos and terror and disported himself amid the sublimity and beauty of nature. Yet gentle as is his mood, he misses not the opportunity, albeit in general he displays an honest leaning towards old superstitions, mercilessly to crush one of the humblest. Do you remember the Priory of St. Ruth, and the summer-party made to visit it, and the preparation for the subsequent rogueries of Dousterswivel in the tale of Martin Waldeck, and the discovery of a spring of water by means of the divining rod?

I am inclined, do you know, to dispute the verdict of the novelist on this occasion, and to take the part of the charlatan against the author of his being; — as far at least as regards the genuineness of the art he then and there affected to practise. There exists in fact strong evidence to shew, that in competent and honest hands the divining rod really does what is pretended of it. This evidence I propose to put before you in the present letter. But as the subject may be entirely new to you, I had best begin by describing what is meant by a divining rod, and in what the imputed jugglery consists.

Then you are to know that in mining districts a superstition prevails among the people, that some are born gifted with an occult power of detecting the proximity of veins of metal and of underground currents of water. In Cornwal they hold that about one in forty possesses this faculty. The mode of exercizing it is very simple. They cut a hazel twig, just below where it forks. Having stripped the leaves off they cut each branch to something more than a foot in length, leaving the stump three inches long. This implement is the divining rod. The hazel is selected for the purpose, because it branches more symmetrically than its neighbours. The hazel-fork is to be held by the branches, one in either hand, the stump or point projecting straight forwards. The arms of the experimenter hang by his sides; but the elbows being bent at a right angle, the fore-arms are advanced; the hands are held seven or eight inches apart, the knuckles down and the thumbs outwards. The ends of the branches of the divining fork appear between the roots of the thumbs and forefingers.

The operator thus armed walks over the ground, he intends exploring, in the full expectation that if he possess the mystic gift, as soon as he passes over a vein of metal or underground spring, the hazel-fork will begin to move spontaneously in his hands, rising or falling as the case may be.

You smile at my gravely stating an event so unlikely. It is indeed natural, that you should suppose the whole a juggle and think the seemingly spontaneous motion of the divining fork to be really communicated to it by the hands of the conjuror; — by a sleight in fact which he puts in practise, when he believes that he is walking over a hidden water-course, or wishes you to believe that there is a vein of metal near. Well, I thought as you do the greater part of my life; and probably the likeliest way of combating your scepticism will be to tell you how my own conversion took place.

In the summer of 1843 I dwelt under the same roof with a Scottish gentleman, well informed, of a serious turn of mind, fully endowed with the national allowance of shrewdness and caution; I saw a good deal of him; and one day by chance this subject of the divining rod was mentioned. He told me, that at one time his curiosity having been raised upon the subject, he had taken pains to ascertain what there is in it. With this object in view he had obtained an introduction to Mrs. R., sister of Sir G. R. then living at Southampton, whom he had learnt to be one of those in whose hands the divining rod moved. He visited the lady, who was polite enough te shew him in what the performance consists, and to answer all his questions and to assist him in making experiments calculated to test the reality of the phenomenon and to elucidate its cause.

Mrs. R. told my friend that being at Cheltenham in 1806 she saw for the first time the divining rod used by Mrs. Colonel Beaumont, who possessed the power of imparting motion to it in a very remarkable degree. Mrs. R. tried the experiment herself at that time, but without any success. She was as it happened very far from well. Afterwards in the year 1815 being asked by a friend how the divining rod is held and how it is to be used, on shewing it she was surprised to see, that the instrument now moved in her hands.

Since then, whenever she had repeated the experiment, the power had always manifested itself tho' with varying degrees of energy.

Mrs. R. then took my friend to a part of the shrubbery where she knew from former trials the divining rod would move in her hands. It did so to my friends extreme astonishment; and even continued to move, when availing himself of Mrs. R's permission, my friend grasped her hands with sufficient firmness to prevent any muscular action of her wrists or fingers, influencing the result.

In a subsequent day my friend having thought over what he had seen, repeated his visit to the lady. He had provided himself as substitutes for the hazel fork which he had seen her employ, with portions of copper and iron-wire about a foot and a half long, bent something into the form of the letter V. He had made in fact divining forks of wire wanting only the projecting point. He found that these instruments moved quite as freely in Mrs. R's hands as the hazel-fork had done. Then he coated the two handles of one of them with sealing wax, leaving however the extreme ends free and uncovered. When Mrs. R. tried the rod so prepared holding the parts alone which were covered with sealing wax, and walked on the same piece of ground as in the former experiments, the rod remained perfectly still. As often however as, with no greater change then adjusting her hands so as to touch the free end of the wire with her thumbs, Mrs. R. renewed direct contact with the instrument, it again moved. The motion ceased again as often as the direct contact was interrupted.

This simple narrative made to me by the late Mr. George Fairholm carried conviction to my mind of the reality of the phenomenon. I asked my friend why he had not pursued the subject further. He said he had often thought of doing so, and had he believed mainly been deterred by meeting with the work of the Compte de Tristan's entitled "Recherches sur quelque effluves terrestres" Paris 1829, in which facts similar to those which he had himself verified were given, and a number of additional curious experiments detailed.

At Mr. Fairholm's instance I procured the book and at a later period read it. I may say that it both satisfied and disappointed me. It satisfied me in as much as it fully confirmed all that Mr. Fairholm had stated. It disappointed me for it threw no additional light upon the phenomena. M. de Tristan had in fact brought too little physical knowledge to the investigation, so that a large proportion of his experiments are a puerile waste of time and ingenuity. However his simpler experiments are valuable, to the point, and good. These I will presently describe. In the mean time you shall hear the count's own narrative of his initiation into the mysteries of the divining rod.

The history of my researches, says M. de Tristan, is simply this. "Some twenty years ago, a gentleman, who from his position in society could have no object to gain by deception, shewed to me for my amusement the movement of the divining rod."

"He attributed the motion to the influence of a current of water, which appeared to me a probable supposition. But my attention was more engaged with the action produced by the influence, let the latter be what it might. My informant assured me he had met with many others, in whom the same effects were manifested. When I was returned home, and had opportunities of making trials under favorable circumstances, I found that I myself possessed the same endowment. Since then I have induced many to make the experiment, and I have found a fourth or certainly a fifth of the number capable of setting the divining rod in motion at the very first attempt. Since that time during these twenty years, I have often tried my hand but for amusement only, and desultorily, and without any idea of making the thing an object of scientific investigation. But at length in the year 1822, being in the country and removed from my ordinary pursuits, the subject again came across me, and I determined forthwith to try and ascertain the cause of these phenomena. Accordingly I commenced a long series of experiments, from fifteen to eighteen hundred in number, which occupied me nearly fifteen months. The results of above twelve hundred were written down at the time of their performance."

The scene of the Count's operations was in the valley of the Loire, five leagues from Vendôme, in the park of the chateau de Ranac. The surface of ground, which gave the desired results, was from seventy to eighty feet in breadth. But there was another spot equally efficient at the Counts ordinary residence at Emerillon, near Clery, four leagues south of Orleans, ten leagues south of the Loire, at the commencement of the plains of Sologne. The surface ran from north to south, and had the same breadth with the other. These "exciting tracts" form in general bands or zones of undetermined and often very great length. Their breadth is very variable. Some are only three or four feet across, while others are one hundred paces. These tracts are sometimes sinuous, in other instances they ramify. To the most susceptible they are broader than to those who are less so.

M. de Tristan thus describes what happens when a competent person, armed with a hazel-fork walks over the exciting districts.

When two or three steps have been made upon the exciting tract of ground, the fork, which at starting is held horizontally, with the point forwards, begins gently to ascend; it gradually attains a vertical position; sometimes it passes beyond that, and lowering itself, with its point to the chest of the operator, it becomes again horizontal. If the motion continues, the rod descending becomes vertical with the point downwards. Finally the rod may again ascend and resume its first position. When the action is very lively, the rod immediately commences a second revolution, and so it goes on, as long as the operator continues to walk over the exciting surface of ground.

A few of those, in whose hands the divining fork moves, exhibit a remarkable peculiarity. The instrument instead of commencing its motion by ascending, descends; the point then becomes directed vertically downwards; afterwards it reascends, and completes a revolution in a course the opposite of the usual one. And as often and as long as its motion is excited, it pursues this abnormal course.

Among the numerous experiments made by M. de Tristan, the following are about the simplest and the best.

He covered both handles of a divining rod with a thick silk stuff. The result of using the instrument so prepared was the same which Mr. Fairholm obtained by coating the handles with sealing wax. The motion of the divining rod was extinguished.

He covered both handles with one layer of a thin silk. He then found that the motion of the divining rod took place, but it was less lively and vigorous than ordinary.

By covering one handle of the divining rod, and that the right, with a layer of thin silk, a very singular and satisfactory result was obtained. The motion of the instrument was now reversed. It commenced by descending.

After covering the point of the divining rod with a thick layer of silk stuff, the motion was sensibly more brisk than it had been before.

When the Count held in his hands a straight rod of the same substance conjointly with the ordinary divining rod, no movement of the latter whatsoever ensued.

Finally the Count discovered that he could cause the divining rod to move, when he walked over a non-exciting surface, as for instance in his own chamber, by various processes. Of these the most interesting consisted in touching the point of the instrument with either pole of a magnetic needle. The instrument shortly began to move, ascending or descending, according as the northward or southward pole of the needle had been applied to it.

It is unnecessary to add that these and all M. de

Tristan's experiments were repeated by him many times. The results of those, which I have narrated, were constant.

Let me now attempt to realize something out of the preceding statements.

1. It appears to me impossible to doubt, upon the testimony adduced, that whereas in the hands of most persons the divining rod remains motionless, in the hands of some it moves promptly and briskly, when the requisite conditions are observed.

2. It appears to me no less certain, that the motion of the divining rod has appeared to various intelligent and honest persons, who have succeeded in producing it, to be entirely spontaneous; or that the said persons were not conscious of having excited or promoted the motion by the slightest help of their own.

3. It appears certain that in the ordinary use of the divining rod by competent persons, its motion only manifests itself in certain localities.

4. It being assumed that the operator does not, however unconsciously, by the muscular action of his hands and wrists produce the motion of the divining rod, the likeliest way of accounting for the phenomenon is to suppose that the divining rod may become made the conductor of some fluid or force, emanating from, or disturbed in the body by, terrestrial agency.

But here a difficulty arises. How can it happen, that the hypothetical force makes so long and round about a course? Why, communicated to the body through the legs, does not the supposed fluid complete a circuit at once in the lower part of the trunk?

Such at all events would be the course an electric current so situated would take.

The difficulty raised admits of being removed by aid derived from a novel and unexpected source. I allude to von Reichenbach's newly discovered principle, which whether or not it be identical with that which gives motion to the divining rod, exhibits at all events the very property, which the hypothetical principle should possess to explain the phenomena, which we have been considering.

No attempts have indeed been made to identify the two as one; and the conjecture that they may prove so, tho' plausible is at the same time so vague that I should have contented myself with referring to von Reichenbach's new principle as to an established truth, and have introduced no account of it into this letter, had I not a second motive for ensuring your cognizance of the curious facts, which the Viennese philosopher has brought to light. It is less with the view of furnishing a leg to the theory of the divining rod, than in order to provide the means of elucidating more interesting problems, that I now proceed briefly to sketch the leading experiments made by von Reichenbach, and their results.

Objections have been taken against these experiments on the ground that they are, with one exception, purely physiological, that the results must be received on the testimony of the subject employed, and that the best subjects for the purpose, are persons whose natural sensibility is exalted by disorder of the nerves. — A class of persons always suspected of exaggeration, and even, and in part with justice, of a tendency to trickery and deception. But this was well known to von Reichenbach, who appears to have taken every precaution necessary to secure his observations against error. And when I add, that many of the results, which he obtained upon the most sensitive and the highly nervous were likewise manifested in persons of established character and in good health; and that the fidelity of the author and of his researches is authenticated by the publication of the latter in Woehler and Liebig's chemical annals (supplement to volume 53, Heidelberg 1845), I think you will not withold from them complete reliance.

In general persons in health and of a strong constitution are totally insensible to the influence of von Reichenbach's new force. But all persons, the tone of whose health has been lowered by their mode of life, men of sedentary habits, clerks and the like, and women who employ their whole time in needle work, whose pale complexions shew the relaxed and therefore irritable state of their frames, — all such or nearly all — evince more or less susceptibility to the influence I am about to describe.

von Reichenbach found that persons of the classes referred to, when slow passes are made with the poles of a strong magnet moved slowly parallel to the surface, — down the back for instance or down the limbs, — and only distant enough just not to touch the clothes, — feel sensations rather unpleasant than otherwise, as of a light draft of air blown upon them in the path of the magnet.

In the progress of his researches von Reichenbach found that his subjects could detect the presence of his new agent by another sense. In the dark they saw dim flames of light issuing and waving from the poles of the magnet. The experiments suggested by this discovery afford the most satisfactory proofs of the reality of the phenomena. — They were the following. A horse-shoe magnet having been adjusted upon a table with the poles directed upwards, the sensitive subject saw, at the distance of ten feet, the appearance of flames issuing from it. The armature of the magnet, — a bar of soft iron — was then applied. Upon this the flames disappeared. They reappeared, she said, as often as the armature was removed from the magnet.

A similar experiment was made with a yet more

sensitive subject. This person saw in the first instance flames as the first had done. But when the armature of the magnet was applied, the flames did not disappear; she saw flames still; only they were fainter and their disposition was different. They seemed now to issue from every part of the surface of the magnet equally.

It is hardly necessary to add that these experiments were made in a well darkened room, and that none of the bystanders could discern what the sensitive subjects saw.

Then the following experiment was made. A powerful lens was so placed, as that it should concentrate the light of the flames, (if real light they were) upon a point of the wall of the room. The patient at once saw the light upon the wall at the right place. And when the inclination of the lens was shifted so as to throw the focus in succession on different points, the sensitive observer never failed in pointing out the right spot.

Next with the assistance of Herr Schuh, an optician in Vienna, a physical experiment was made, which seems to remove all doubt of the identity of these to-common eyes-invisible flames with common light. A prepared daguerrotype plate was kept in due opposition to the poles of a strong magnet for sixty four hours in perfect darkness. At the expiration of that time the plate was found to exhibit the fullest influence of light upon its whole surface.

To his new force, which von Reichenbach had now found to emanate likewise from the poles of crystals and the wires of the Voltaic pile, he gave the name of Od, or the Od force.

His next step was to ascertain the existence of a difference among the sensations produced by Od. Sometimes the current of air was described as warm, sometimes as cool. He found this difference to depend upon the following cause. Whenever the northward pole of a magnet, or one definite pole of a large crystal, or the negative wire of a voltaic battery, is employed in the experiment, the sensation produced is that of a draft of cool air. On the contrary the southward pole of the magnet, the opposite pole of the crystal, the positive voltaic wire, excite the sensation of a draft of warm air.

So the new force appeared to be a polar force, and von Reichenbach called the first series of the above described manifestations *Od-negative* effects, the second *Od-positive* effects.

From among his numerous experiments towards establishing the polarity of Od I select the following. One of the most sensitive of his subjects held, at his desire, a piece of copper wire, by the middle with the right hand, by one end with the left. Then von Reichenbach touched the free end of the wire with one pole of a large crystal in order to charge it with Od. The patient immediately felt a sensation in the right hand; which disappeared as quickly, to be felt by the left hand instead, at the further end of the piece of wire. She then was bidden to take hold of the wire with both her hands at the middle, and then to slide them away from each other to the opposite ends; she observed on doing so that sensations were produced, which were strong and decided, when her hands held the two ends of the wire, and diminished in intensity in proportion as the hands were nearer its middle.

von Reichenbach next came upon the observation that the human hand gives out the Od force; and that the right hand displays the characters of negative Od, the left those of positive Od. The more sensitive subjects recognized, in the dark, the appearance of dim flames proceeding from the tips of his fingers: and all felt the corresponding sensations of drafts of cool or of warm air. Subsequently the whole body was found to share the properties of the hands; the entire right side to manifest negative Od, the entire left side positive Od.

So in reference to this new force the human body exhibits a transverse polarity; the condition is thus realized, which is required to belong to the hypothetical force, through which the divining rod might be supposed to move. If any terrestrial influence were capable of disturbing the Od force in the body, however it might affect its intensity, a current or circuit could only be established through the arms and hands; unless indeed some extraordinary means were taken, such as employing an artificial conductor, arched half round the body, to connect the two sides.

The sensations, which attend the establishment of a current of Od and interferences with it, in sensitive subjects, are exemplified in the following observations.

A bar-magnet was laid on the palm of the left hand of one of the most sensitive subjects, with its southward pole resting on the end of her middle finger; the northward pole on the fore-arm above the wrist. It thus corresponded with the natural polar arrangement of the Od force in the patients hand and arm. Accordingly no sensation was excited. But when the position of the magnet was reversed, and the northward-pole lay on the end of the middle finger of the left hand, an uneasy sense of an inward conflict arose in the hand and wrist, which disappeared, when the magnet was removed or its original direction restored. On laying the magnet reversed on the fore-arm the sense of an inward struggle returned; which was heightened on joining the hands and establishing a circuit.

When the patient completed the circuit in another way, namely by holding a bar-magnet by the ends, — if the latter were disposed normally, that is, if the northward pole was held in the left hand, the southward pole in the right, a lively consciousness of some inward action ensued. A normal circulation of Od was in progress. When the direction of the magnet was reversed, the phenomenon mentioned in the last paragraph recurred. The patient experienced a high degree of uneasiness, a feeling as of an inward struggle extending itself to the chest, with a sense of whirling round and confusion in the head. These symptoms disappeared immediately upon her leaving go of the magnet.

Similar results ensued, when von Reichenbach substituted himself for the magnet. When he took Miss Maix's hands in his, normally, that is to say, her left in his right, her right in his left, she felt a circulation moving up the right arm through the chest down the left arm, attended with a sense of giddiness. When he changed hands, the disagreeableness of the sensation was suddenly heightened, the sense of inward conflict arose, attended with a sort of undulation up and down the arms and through the chest, which quickly became intolerable.

A singular but consistent difference in the result ensued, when von Reichenbach repeated the two last experiments upon Herr Schuh. Herr Schuh was a strong man, thirty years of age, in full health, but highly impressionable by Od. When von Reichenbach took his two hands in his own normally, Herr Schuh felt the normal establishment of the Od current in his arms and chest. In a few seconds headache and vertigo ensued, and the experiment was too disagreeable to be prolonged. But when von Reichenbach took his hands abnormally, no sensible effect ensued. Being equally strong with von Reichenbach, Herr Schuh's frame repelled the counter-current, which the latter arrangement tended to throw into him. In the first or normal arrangement the od current had met with no resistance, but had simply gone its natural course. The distress occurred *from its being felt,* through Herr Schuh's accidental sensitiveness to Od; of the freaks of which in their systems people in general are unconscious.

I have concluded my case in favor of the pretensions of the divining rod. It seems to me at all events strong enough to justify any one who has leisure, in cutting a hazel-fork and walking about with it in suitable places, holding it in the manner described. I doubt, however, whether I should recommend a friend to make the experiment. If by good luck the divining rod should refuse to move in his hands, he might accuse himself of credulity, and feel silly, and hope nobody had seen him for the rest of the day. If unfortunately the first trial should succeed and he should be led to pursue the inquiry, the consequences would be more serious; his probable fate would be to fall at once several degrees in the estimation of his friends, and to pass with the world, all the rest of his life, for a crotchetty person of weak intellects.

As for the divining rod itself, if my argument prove sound, it will be a credit to the family of superstitions. For without any reduction, or clipping, or trimming, it may at once assume the rank of a new truth. But alas, the trials, which await it in that character! — what an ordeal is before it. A new truth has to encounter three normal stages of opposition. In the first, it is denounced as an imposture. In the second, that is, when it is beginning to force itself into notice, it is cursorily examined and plausibly explained away. In the third, or "cui bono" stage, it is decried as useless, and hostile to religion. And when it is finally admitted, it passes only under a protest that is has been perfectly known for ages — a proceeding intended to make the new truth ashamed of itself, and wish it had never been born.

I congratulate the sea-serpent on having arrived at the second stage of belief. Since Professor Owen (no disrespect to his genuine ability and eminent knowledge) has explained it into a sea — elephant, its chance of being itself is much improved; and as it will skip the third stage, for who will venture to question the good of a sea-serpent, it is liable now any morning "to wake and find itself famous;" and to be received even at Lincoln's Inn field's, where its remains may commemoratively be ticketted the Ex-Great-Seal.

Letter II

VAMPYRISM

In acknowledging my former letter you express an eager desire to learn, as you phrase it "all about vampyrs if there ever were such things," I will not delay satisfying your curiosity, altho' by so doing I interrupt the logical order of my communications. It is perhaps all the better. The proper place of this subject falls in the midst of a philosophical disquisition; and it would have been a pity not to present it to you in its pristine coloring. But how came your late tutor, Mr. H., to leave you in ignorance upon a point, on which in my time schoolboys much your juniors entertained decided opinions.

Were there ever such things as Vampyrs? *tantamne rem tam negligenter!* I turn to the learned pages of Horst for a luminous and precise definition of the destructive and mysterious beings, whose existence you have ventured to consider problematical.

"A Vampyr is a dead body, which continues to live in the grave, which it leaves however by night, for the purpose of sucking the blood of the living, whereby it is nourished, and preserved in good condition, instead of becoming decomposed like other dead bodies."

Upon my word you really deserve, since Mr. George Combe has clearly shewn in his admirable work on the constitution of man and its adaptation to the surrounding world, that ignorance is a statutable crime before nature and punished by the laws of Providence — you deserve I say, unless you contrive to make Mr. H. your substitute, which I think would be just, yourself to be the subject of the nocturnal visit of a Vampyr. Your scepticism will abate pretty considerably, when you see him stealthily entering your room, yet are powerless under the fascination of his fixed and leaden eye — when you are conscious, as you lie motionless with terror, of his nearer and nearer approach, — when you feel his face, fresh with the smell of the grave, bent over your throat, while his keen teeth make a fine incision in your jugular, preparatorily to his commencing his plain but nutritive repast.

You would look a little paler the next morning, but that would be all for the moment: for Fischer informs us, that the bite of a Vampyr leaves in general no mark upon the person. But he fearfully adds, "it (the bite) is nevertheless speedily fatal," unless the bitten person protect himself by eating some of the earth from the grave of the Vampyr, and smearing himself with his blood. Unfortunately indeed these measures are only of temporary use. Fischer adds, "if through these precautions the life of the victim be prolonged for a period, sooner or later he ends with becoming a Vampyr himself; that is to say, he dies and is buried, but continues to lead a Vampyr life in the grave, nourishing himself by infecting others and promiscuously propagating Vampyrism."

This is no romancer's dream. It is a succinct account of a superstition, which to this day survives in the east of Europe where little more than a century ago it was frightfully prevalent. At that period Vampyrism spread like a pestilence through Servia and Wallachia, causing numerous deaths, and disturbing all the land with fear of the mysterious visitation, against which no one felt himself secure.

Here is something like a good solid practical popular delusion. Do I believe it? to be sure I do; the facts are matter of history; the people died like sheep, and the cause and method of their dying was in their belief, what has just been stated. You suppose, then, they died frightened out of their lives; as men have died, whose pardon has been proclaimed when their necks were already on the block, of the belief they were going to die? well if that were all, the subject would be worth examining: but there is more in it than that; as the following o'er true tale will convince you, the essential points of which are authenticated by documentary evidence.

In the spring of 1727 there returned from the Levant to the village of Meduegna near Belgrade, one Arnod Paole, who in a few years of military service and varied adventure, had amassed enough to purchase a cottage and an acre or two of land in his native place, where he gave out that he meant to pass the remainder of his days. He kept his word. Arnod had yet scarcely reached the prime of manhood; and though he must have encountered the rough as well as the smooth of life, and have mingled with many a wild and reckless companion, yet his naturally good disposition and honest principles had preserved him unscathed in the scenes he had passed through. At all events such were the thoughts expressed by his neighbours, as they discussed his return and settlement among them in the Stube of the village Hof. Nor did the frank and open countenance of Arnod, his obliging habits, and steady conduct, argue their judgment incorrect. Nevertheless, there was something occasionally noticeable in his ways, a look and tone, that betrayed inward disquiet. Often would he refuse to join his friends, or on some sudden plea abruptly quit their society. And he still more unaccountably, and as it seemed systematically, avoided meeting his pretty neighbour, Nina, whose father occupied the next tenement to his own. At the age of seventeen Nina was as charming a picture as you could have seen, of youth, cheerfulness, innocence, and confidence in all the world. You could not look into her limpid eyes, which steadily returned your gaze, without seeing to the bottom of the pure and transparent spring of her thoughts. Why then did Arnod shrink from meeting her? He was young, had a little property, had health and industry, and he had told his friends he had formed no ties in other lands. Why, then, did he avoid the fascination of the pretty Nina, who seemed a being made to chase from any brow the clouds of gathering care? But he did so. Yet less and less resolutely; for he felt the charm of her presence; who could have done otherwise? and how could he long resist — he did'nt — the impulse of his fondness for the innocent girl, who often sought to cheer his fits of depression.

And they were to be united; were betrothed; yet still an anxious gloom would fitfully overcast his countenance even in the sun-shine of those hours.

"What is it, dear Arnod, that makes you sad? it cannot be on my account, I know; for you were sad before you ever noticed me; and that I think," and you should have seen the deepening rose upon her cheeks, "surely first made me notice you."

"Nina," he answered, "I have done, I fear, a great wrong, in trying to gain your affections — Nina, I have a fixed impression that I shall not live; — yet knowing this, I have selfishly made my existence necessary to your happiness"

"How strangely you talk, dear Arnod; who in the village is stronger and healthier than you? You feared no danger when you were a soldier? what danger do you fear as a villager of Meduegna?"

"It haunts me, Nina."

"But Arnod you were sad before you thought of me; did you then fear to die?"

"Ah, Nina, it is something worse than death." And his vigorous frame shook with agony.

"Arnod, I conjure you, tell me."

"It was in Cossova this fate befell me, — here you have hitherto escaped the terrible scourge. But there they died, and the dead visited the living. I experienced the first frightful visitation, and I fled; but not till I had sought his grave and exacted the dread expiation from the Vampyr."

Nina's blood ran cold. She stood horrorstricken. But her young heart soon mastered her first despair. With a touching voice she spoke: —

"Fear not, dear Arnod, fear not now. I will be your shield, — or I will die with you."

And she encircled his neck with her gentle arms; and returning hope shone, Iris-like, amid her falling tears. Afterwards they found a reasonable ground for banishing or allaying their apprehensions, in the length of time, which had elapsed since Arnod left Cossova, during which no fearful visitant had again approached him; and they fondly trusted *that* gave them security.

It is a strange world. The ills we fear are commonly not those which overwhelm us. The blows that reach us are for the most part unforeseen. One day about a week after this conversation, Arnod missed his footing, when on the top of a loaded hay-waggon, and fell from it to the ground. He was picked up insensible, and carried home, where after lingering a short time he died; his interment as usual followed immediately: — his fate was sad and premature; but what pencil could paint Nina's grief?

Twenty or thirty days after his decease, says the perfectly authenticated report of these transactions, several of the neighbourhood complained that they were haunted by the deceased Arnod; and what was more to the purpose, four of them died. The evil looked at sceptically was bad enough; but aggravated by the suggestions of superstition, it spread a panic through the whole district. To allay the popular terror, and if possible to get at the root of the evil, a determination was come to publicly to disinter the body of Arnod with the view of ascertaining whether he really was a Vampyr; and in that event of treating him comfortably. The day fixed for this proceeding was the fortieth after his burial.

It was on a grey morning in early August that the commission visited the quiet cemetery of Meduegna, which surrounded with a wall of unhewn stone, lies sheltered by the mountain that rising in undulating green slopes irregularly planted with fruit trees, ends in an abrupt craggy ridge feathered with under-wood. The graves were for the most part neatly kept, with borders of box or something like it, and flowers between; and at the head of most, a small wooden cross painted black bearing the name of the tenant. Here and there a stone had been raised; one of considerable height, a single narrow slab, ornamented with grotesque gothic carvings dominated over the rest. Near this lay the grave of Arnod Paole, towards which the party moved. The work of throwing out the earth was begun by the grey crooked old sexton, who lived in the Leichenhouse beyond the great crucifix; he seemed unconcerned enough; no Vampyr would think of extracting a supper out of him. Nearest the grave stood two military surgeons or feldscheerers, from Belgrade, and a drummer-boy, who held their case of instruments. The boy looked on with keen interest; and when the coffin was exposed, and rather roughly drawn out of the grave, his pale face and bright intent eye shewed how the scene moved him. The sexton lifted the lid of the coffin; the body had become inclined to one side; when turning it straight "ha" "ha" said he pointing to fresh blood upon the lips, "ha" "ha" what, your mouth not wiped since last night's work?" the spectators shuddered: the drummer-boy sank forward fainting and upset the instrument case scattering its contents; the senior surgeon infected with the horror of the scene repressed a hasty exclamation and simply crossed himself. They threw water on the drummer-boy and he recovered but would not leave the spot. Then they inspected the body of Arnod. It looked is if it had not been dead a day. On handling it the scarfskin came off, but below were *new skin and new nails!* How could *they* have come there, but from its foul feeding? The case was clear enough; there lay before them the thing they dreaded — the Vampyr. So without more ado they simply drove a stake through poor Arnod's chest; whereupon a quantity of blood gushed forth and the corpse uttered an audible groan. — "Murder, Oh Murder," — shrieked the drummer-boy, as he rushed wildly with convulsed gestures from the cemetery.

The drummer-boy was not far from the mark. — But quitting the romancing vein which had led me to try and restore the original colours of the picture, let me confine myself in describing the rest of the scene and what followed, to the words of my authority.

The body of Arnod was then burnt to ashes, which were returned to the grave. The authorities farther had staked and burnt the bodies of the four others, which were supposed to have been infected by Arnod; no mention is made of the state in which they were found. The adoption of these decisive measures failed however of entirely extinguishing the evil, which continued still to hang about the village. About five years afterwards it had again become very rife and many died through it. Whereupon the authorities determined to make another and a complete clearance of the Vampyrs in the cemetery; and with that object they had again all the graves to which present suspicion attached, opened and their contents officially anatomized, of which procedure the following is the medical report, here and there *abridged* only; —

1. a woman of the name of Stana, twenty years of age who had died three months before of a three days illness following her confinement. She had before her death avowed that she had *anointed* herself with the blood of a vampyr, to liberate herself from his persecution. Nevertheless, she as well as her infant, whose body through careless interment had been half eaten by the dogs, both had died. Her body was entirely free from decomposition. On opening it the chest was found full of recently effused blood, and the bowels had exactly the appearances of sound health. The skin and nails of her hands and feet were loose and came off, but underneath lay new skin and nails.

2. A woman of the name of Miliza, who had died

at the end of a three months illness. The body had been buried ninety and odd days. In the chest was liquid blood. The viscera were as in the former instance. The body was declared by a heyduk who recognized it, to be in better condition and fatter than it had been in the woman's legitimate life-time.

3. The body of a child eight years old, that had likewise been buried ninety days; it was in the Vampyr condition.

4. The son of a heyduk named Milloc, sixteen years old. The body had lain in the grave nine weeks. He had died after three days indisposition and was in the condition of a Vampyr.

5. Joachim, likewise son of a heyduk, seventeen years old. He had died after three days illness; had been buried eight weeks and some days; was found in the Vampyr state.

6. A woman of the name of Rusha, who had died of an illness of ten days duration, and had been six weeks buried, in whom likewise fresh blood was found in the chest.

(The reader will understand, that to *see* blood in the chest, it is first necessary to *cut* the chest open.)

7. The body of a girl of ten years of age, who had died two months before. It was likewise in the vampyr state, perfectly undecomposed, with blood in the chest.

8. The body of the wife of one Hadnuck, buried seven weeks before; and that of her infant eight weeks old, buried only twenty one days. They were both in a state of decomposition, tho' buried in the same ground and closely adjoining the others.

9. A servant by name Rhade, twenty three years of age; he had died after an illness of three months dura-

tion, and the body had been buried five weeks. It was in a state of decomposition.

10. The body of the heyduk, Stanco, sixty years of age, who had died six weeks previously. There was much blood and other fluid in the chest and abdomen, and the body was in the Vampyr condition.

11. Millac, a heyduk, twenty five years old. The body had been in the earth six weeks. It was perfectly in the vampyr condition.

12. Stanjoika, the wife of a heyduk, twenty years old; had died after an illness of three days, and had been buried eighteen. The countenance was florid. There was blood in the chest and in the heart. The viscera were perfectly sound: the skin remarkably fresh.

The document, which gives the above particulars, is signed by three regimental Surgeons and formally countersigned by a lieutenant-colonel and sub-lieutenant; it bears the date of June 7. 1732, Meduegna near Belgrade. No doubt can be entertained of its authenticity or of its *general* fidelity; the less that it does not stand alone, but is supported by a mass of evidence to the same effect. It appears to establish beyond question, that where the fear of vampyrism prevails and there occur several deaths, in the popular belief connected with it, the bodies, when disinterred weeks after burial, present the appearance of corpses from which life has only recently departed.

What inference shall we draw from this fact? — that vampyrism is true in the popular sense; and that these fresh-looking and well-conditioned corpses had some mysterious source of praeternatural nurrishment? That would be to adopt, not to solve the superstition. Let us content ourselves with a notion not so monstrous, but still startling enough. — That the bodies, which were found in the so-called vampyr-state, instead of being in a new or mystical condition, were simply alive in the common way, or had been so for sometime subsequently to their interment; that, in short, they were the bodies of persons who had been buried alive, and whose life, where it yet lingered, was finally extinguished through the ignorance and barbarity of those who disinterred them. In the following sketch of a similar scene to that above described, the correctness of this inference comes out with terrific force.

Erasmus Francisci, in his remarks upon the description of the Dukedom of Krain by Valvasor, speaks of a man of the name of Grando, in the district of Kring, who died, was buried, and became a Vampyr, and as such was exhumed for the purpose of having a stake thrust through him.

> "When they opened his grave, after he had been long buried, his face was found with a colour, and his features made natural sorts of movements, as if the dead man smiled. He even opened his mouth as if he would inhale fresh air. They held the crucifix before him, and called in a loud voice, "See, this is Jesus Christ who redeemed your soul from hell, and died for you." After the sound had acted on his organs of hearing, and he had connected perhaps some ideas with it, tears began to flow from the dead man's eyes. Finally, when after a short prayer for his poor soul they proceeded to hack off his head, the corpse uttered a screech, and turned and rolled just as if it had been alive, and the grave was full of blood."

We have thus succeeded in interpreting one of the unknown terms in the vampyr-theorem. The suspicious character, who had some dark way of nourishing himself in the grave, turns out to be an unfortunate gentleman (or lady) whom his friends had in ignorance buried, while he was still alive; and who, if they afterwards mercifully let him alone, died sooner or later either naturally or of the primature interment, — in either case it is to be hoped with no interval of restored consciousness. The state, which thus passed for death and led to such fatal consequences, apart from superstition deserves our serious consideration. For altho' of very rare it is of continual occurrence, and society is not sufficiently on its guard against a contingency so dreadful when overlooked. When the nurse or the doctor has announced that all is over, — that the valued friend or relative has breathed his last — no doubt crosses any one's mind of the reality of the sad event. Disease is now so well understood, every step in its march laid down and foreseen, the approach of danger accurately estimated, the liability of the patient according to his powers of resisting it, to succumb earlier or to hold out longer; all is theoretically so clear, that a wholesome suspicion of error in the verdict of the attendants seldom suggests itself. The evil I am considering ought not however to be attributed to redundance of knowledge; it arises from its partial lack, from a too general neglect of one very important section in pathological science. The laity, if not the doctors too, constantly lose sight of the fact, that there exists an alternative to the fatal event of ordinary disease; that a patient is liable at any period of illness to deviate, or as it were to slide off, from the customary line of disease into another and a deceptive route, — *instead of death, to encounter apparent death.*

The Germans have an excellent term for this condition of the living body; they call it "Scheintod," which signifies simply apparent death. The english language is not malleable enough to admit of the invention of a similar term. But the term death-trance is a very tolerable equivalent.

Death-trance is a form of suspended animation. There are several others. After incomplete poisoning, after suffocation in either of its various ways, after exposure to cold, in infants newly born, a state is occasionally met with, of which (however each may still differ from the rest) the common feature is an apparent suspension of the vital actions. But all of these so-cited instances agree in another important respect; which second inter-agreement separates them as a class from death-trance. They represent, each and all, a period of conflict between the effects of certain deleterious impressions and the vital principle, the latter struggling against the weight and force of the former. Such is not the case in death-trance.

Death-trance is a positive status; a period of repose; the duration of which is sometimes definite and predetermined, tho' unknown. Thus the patient, the term of the death-trance having expired, occasionally suddenly wakes, entirely and at once restored. Oftener, however, the machinery which has been stopped seems to require to be jogged; then it goes on again.

The basis of death-trance is suspension of the action of the heart, and of the breathing, and of voluntary motion: generally likewise feeling and intelligence, and the vegetative changes in the body, are suspended. With these phenomena is joined loss of external warmth; so that the usual evidence of life is gone. But there has occurred every shade of this condition that can be imagined between occasional slight manifestations of one or other of the vital actions, and their entire disparition.

Death-trance may occur as a primary affection suddenly or gradually. The diseases the course of which it is liable, as it were, to bifurcate, or to graft itself upon are first and principally all disorders of the nervous system. But in any form of disease, when the body is brought to a certain degree of debility, death-trance may supervene. Age and sex have to do with its occurence; which is more frequent in the young than in the old, in men than in women; — differences evidently connected with greater irritability of nervous system. Accordingly women in labor are among the most liable to death-trance, and it is from such a case that I will give a first instance of the affection as pourtrayed by a medical witness. (Journal des Savans 1749.)

M. Rigaudeaux, surgeon to the military hospital and licensed accoucheur at Douai, was sent for on the 8th of september 1745, to attend the wife of Francis Dumont residing two leagues from the town. He was late in getting there, it was half past 8 a. m., too late it seemed; the patient was declared to have died at 6 o'clock, after eighteen hours of ineffectual labor-pains. M. Rigaudeaux inspected the body; there was no pulse or breath; the mouth was full of froth; the abdomen tumid. He brought away the infant, which he committed to the care of the nurses; who after trying to reanimate it for three hours gave up the attempt, and prepared to lay it out; when it opened its mouth. They then gave it wine and it was speedily recovered. M. Rigaudeaux, who returned to the house as this occurred, inspected again the body of the mother. (It had been already nailed down in a coffin.) He examined it with the utmost care; but he came to the conclusion that it was certainly dead. Nevertheless as the joints of the limbs were still flexible, altho' seven hours had elapsed since its apparent death, he left the strictest injunctions, to watch the body carefully, to apply stimulants to the nostrils from time to time, to slap the palms of the hands, and the like. At half past three o'clock symptoms of returning animation shewed themselves, and the patient recovered.

The period during which every ordinary sign of life may be absent, without the prevention of their return, is unknown, but in well authenticated cases it has much exceeded the period observed in the above instance. Here is an example, borrowed from the "journal des Savans" 1741.

There was a Colonel Russel, whose wife, to whom he was affectionately attached, died, or appeared to do so. But he would not allow the body to be buried; and threatened to shoot any one who should interfere to remove it for that purpose. His conduct was guided by reason as well as affection and instinct. He said the would not part from the body till its decomposition had begun. Eight days had passed during which the body of his wife gave no sign of life; — when, as he sat bedewing her hand with his tears, the churchbell tolled, and to his unspeakable amazement, his wife sat up, and said "that is the last bell, we shall be too late." She recovered.

There are cases on record of persons, who could spontaneously fall into death-trance. — Monti in a letter to Haller adverts to several; and mentions in particular, a peasant upon whom, when he assumed this state, the flies would settle; breathing, the pulse, and all ordinary signs of life disappeared.

A priest of the name of Caelius Rhodaginus had the same faculty; but the most celebrated instance is that of Colonel Townshend, mentioned in the surgical works of Gooch; by whom and by Doctor Cheyne and Doctor Baynard, and by Mr. Shrine, an apothecary, the perfornance of Colonel Townshend was seen and attested. They had long attended him, for he was an habitual invalid; and he had often invited them to witness the phenomenon of his dying and coming to life again, but they had hitherto refused from fear of the consequences to himself. But at last they assented. Accordingly in their presence Colonel Townshend laid himself down on his back, and Doctor Cheyne undertook to observe his pulse; Doctor Baynard laid his hand on his heart; and Mr. Shrine had a looking glass to hold to his mouth. After a few seconds, pulse, breathing and the action of the heart, were no longer to be observed. Each of the witnesses satisfied himself of the entire cessation of these phenomena. When the death-trance had lasted half an hour, the Doctors began to fear that their patient had pushed the experiment too far and was dead in earnest. And they were preparing to leave the house, when a slight movement of the body attracted their attention. They renewed their routine of observation; when the pulse and sensible motion of the heart gradually returned, and breathing, and consciousness. The sequel of the tale is strange. Colonel Townshend on recovering sent for his attorney, made his will, and died, for good and all, six hours afterwards.

Although many have recovered from death-trance, and there seems to be in each case a definite period to its duration, yet its event is not always as fortunate. The patient sometimes really dies during its continuance, whether unavoidably, or in consequence of adequate measures not being taken to stimulate him to waken, or to support life. The following very good instance rests on the authority of Doctor Schmidt, a physician of the hospital of Paderborn, where it occured. Rheinisch-Westphälischer Anzeiger 1835. N° 57 und 58.

A young man of the name of Caspar Kreite from Berne died in the hospital of Paderborn, but his body could not be interred for three weeks for the following reasons. During the first twenty four hours after drawing its last breath the corpse opened its eyes, and the pulse could be felt for a few minutes beating feebly and irregularly. On the third and fourth day points of the skin, which had been burned, to test the reality of his death, suppurated. On the fifth day the corpse changed the position of one hand; on the ninth day a vesiculal eruption appeared on the back. For nine days there was a vertical fold of the skin of the forehead, a sort of frown; and the features had not the character of death. The lips remained red till the eighteenth day; and the joints preserved their flexibility from first to last. He lay in this state in a warm room for nineteen days without any farther alteration than a sensible wasting in flesh. Till after the nineteenth day no discolorations of the body or odor of putrefaction were observed. He had been cured of ague; and laboured under a slight chest affection, but there had been no adequate cause for his death. It is evident, that this person was much more alive than many are in the death-trance; and one half suspects that stimulants and nourishment properly introduced might have entirely reanimated him.

I might examplify death-trance by many a well authenticated romantic story; — a noise heard in a vault; the people instead of breaking open the door go for the keys and for authority to act, and return too late; the unfortunate person is found dead, having previously gnawn her hand and arm in agony. — A lady is buried with a jewel of value on her finger; thieves open the vault to possess themselves of the treasure; the ring can not be drawn from the finger and the thieves proceed to cut the finger off; the lady wakening from her trance scares the thieves away and recovers. A young married lady dies and is buried; a former admirer, to whom her parents had refused her hand, bribes the sexton to let him see once more the form he loved. The body opportunely comes to life at this moment, and flies from Paris with its first lover to England, where they are married. Venturing to return to France, the lady is recognized, and is reclaimed by her previous husband through a suit at law; her counsel demurs on the ground of the desertion and burial; but the law not admitting this plea, she flies again to England with her preserver, to avoid the judgment of the parliament of Paris, in the acts of which the case stands recorded. There are one or two other cases that I dare not cite, the particulars of which transcend the wildest flights of imagination.

It may be thought that these are all tales of the olden time; and that the very case I have given from the hospital at Paderborn shews that now medical men are sufficiently circumspect, and the public really on its guard to prevent a living person being interred as one dead. And I grant that in England among all but the poorest class the danger is practically inconsiderable of being buried alive. But that it still exists for every class, and that for the poor the danger is great and serious, I am afraid there is too much reason for believing. It is stated in Froriep's Notizen 1829, Nro. 522, that agreeably to a then recent ordinance in New York, coffins presented for burial were kept above ground eight days, open at the head, and so arranged, that the least movement of the body would ring a bell, through strings attached to the hands and feet. It will hardly be credited that *out of twelve hundred* whose interment had been then postponed, *six returned to life,* one in every two hundred! The arrangement thus beneficently adopted at New York is, however, imperfect, as it makes time the criterion for interment. The time is *not* known, during which a body in death-trance may remain alive. Nothing but one positive condition of the body, which I will presently mention, authenticates death. It is frightful to think how in the south of Europe, within twenty four hours after the last breath, bodies are shovelled into pits among heaped corpses; and to imagine what fearful agonies of despair must sometimes be encountered by unhappy beings, who wake amid the unutterable horrors of such a grave. But it is enough to look at home and to make no delay in providing there for the careful watching of the bodies of the poor, till life has certainly departed. Many do not dream how barbarous and backward the vaunted nineteenth century will appear to posterity!

But there is another danger, to which society is obnoxious through not making sufficient account of the contingency of death-trance, that appears to me more urgent and menacing, than even the risk of being buried alive.

The danger I advert to is not *this*; but this is something; —

The cardinal Espinosa, prime minister under Philip the second of Spain, died as it was supposed, after a short illness. His rank entitled him to be embalmed. Accordingly the body was opened for that purpose. The lungs and heart had just been brought into view, when the latter was seen to beat. The cardinal awakening at the fatal moment had still strength enough left to seize with his hand the knife of the anatomist!

But it is *this*; —

On the 23 of september 1763, the abbé Prevost, the french novelist and compiler of travels was seized with a fit in the wood of Chantilly. The body was found and conveyed to the residence of the nearest clergyman. It was supposed that death had taken place through apoplexy. But the local authorities, desiring to be satisfied of the fact, ordered the body to be examined. During the process the poor abbé uttered a cry of agony; — it was too late.

It is to be observed that cases of sudden and unexplained death are on the one hand the cases most likely to furnish a large per-centage of death-trance; and on the other are just those, in which the anxiety of friends or the overzealousness of a coroner is liable to lead to premature anatomization. Nor does it even follow that because the body happily did not wake while being dissected, the spark of life was therefore extinct. But this view is too painful to be followed out in reference to the past. But it imperatively suggests the necessity of forbidding necroscopic examinations, before there is perfect evidence that life has departed; — that is, of extending to this practice the rule, which ought to be made absolute in reference to interment.

Thus comes out the practical importance of the question, how is it to be known that the body is no longer alive?

The entire absence of the ordinary signs of life is insufficient to prove the absence of life. The body may be externally cold; the pulse not to be felt; breathing may have ceased; no bodily motion may occur; the limbs may be stiff (through spasm); the sphincter muscles relaxed; no blood may flow from an opened vein; the eyes may have become glassy; there may be partial *mortification* to offend the sense with the smell of death; — and yet the body may be alive.

The only security we **at present** know of that life has left the body, is the supervention of chemical decomposition, shewn in commencing change of colour of the integuments of the abdomen and throat to blue and green, and an attendant cadaverous fœtor.

To return from this important digression to the feebler subject of the Vampyr-superstition. The second element which we have yet to explain in the letter is the Vampyr-visit, and its consequence, — the lapse of the party visited into death-trance. There are two ways of dealing with this knot; one is to cut it, the other to untye it.

It may be cut, by denying the supposed connexion between the vampyr-visit and the supervention of death-trance in the second party. Nor is the explanation thus obtained devoid of plausibility. There is no reason why death-trance should not in certain seasons and places be *epidemic.* Then the persons most liable to it would be those of weak and irritable nervous systems. Again a first effect of the epidemic might be further to shake the nerves of weaker subjects. These are exactly the persons, who are likely to be infected with imaginary terrors, and to dream, or even to fancy they have seen, Mr. or Mrs. such a one, the last victims of the epidemic. The dream or impression upon the senses might again recur, and the sickening patient have already talked of it to his neighbours, before he himself was seized with death-trance. On this supposition the vampyr-visit would sink into the subordinate rank of a mere premonitory symptom.

To myself, I must confess, this explanation, the best I am yet in a position to offer, appears barren and jejune; and not at all to do justice to the force and frequency, or, as tradition represents the matter, the universality of the vampyr-visit as a precursor of the victim's fate. Imagine how strong must have been the conviction of the reality of the apparition, how common a feature it must have been, to have led to the laying down of the unnatural and repulsive process customarily followed at the Vampyr's grave, as the regular and proper and only preventive of ulterior consequences.

I am disposed therefore rather to try and untye this knot, and with that object to wait, — hoping that something may turn up in the progress of these inquiries to assist me in its solution. In the mean time I would beg leave to consider this second half of the problem a compound phenomenon, the solutions of the two parts of which may not emerge simultaneously. The vampyr-visit is one thing; its presumed contagious effect another.

The vampyr-visit! well, it is clear the vampyr could not have left his grave bodily, or at all events if he could, he never could have buried himself again. Yet there they always found him. So the body could not have been the visitant. Then in popular language it was the ghost of the vampyr that haunted its future victim. The ghostly nature of the visitant could not have been identified at a luckier moment. The very subject, which I next propose to undertake is the analysis of ghosts I have therefore only to throw the vampyr-ghost into the crucible with the rest; and tomorrow I may perhaps be able to report the rational composition of the whole batch.

Letter III

UNREAL GHOSTS

The projected analysis has been crowned with success. The fumes of superstition have been driven off; and the ghosts have been reduced to rational elements. All trace of supernatural agency has vanished; and in its place are found three principles, one physical, two psychical, by the help of which every conceivable ghost may in future be alternately decomposed and recomposed by the merest tyro.

The first, of which I shall describe the nature and operation, is a psychical truth already known to most persons of education. It is of very general use in ghost-building. It forms the immediate personnel of every ghost; and is of so active a nature, that alone, or assisted by a little credulity, it is enough to constitute the simplest kind of ghost, a common fetch. Mixed with a dose of mental anxiety, or as much remorse as will lie on the point of a dagger, it will form a troublesome retrospective ghost. The second principle, a physical one, less generally known, is the basis of that sturdy apparition the church-yard ghost; — which it will turn out in very fair style aided by fancy alone, but to perfect the illusive result the cooperation of the first principle is necessary. The third, an entirely new one, is the foundation of real ghosts, that is of ghosts which announce unexpected events, distant in space or time: the same principle is concerned in true dreams and in second sight.

The first of the three principles adverted to is the physiological fact, that, when the blood is heated, the nervous system overstrained, or digestion out of sorts, the thereby directly or sympathetically disordered brain projects before us illusory forms, coloured and moving like life, and so far undistinguishable from reality. Sometimes a second sense is drawn into the phantasmagoria, and the fictitious beings speak as you do. Almost always the illusion stops there. But in one or two marvellous cases the touch has been involved in the hallucination, and the ghost has been tangible. The phenomena are termed sensorial illusions. The visual part of them, the first and commonest has been the most attended to. The cause immediately producing it appears to be an affection, not of the organ of vision, but of that part of the brain in which the nerves of seeing take their origin. This organ it is which in health realizes our sensations of colour, and converts them into visual perceptions. Like other parts of the brain it is stored with memories of its past impressions, ready to be called up, either pure and true by conception, or any how combined by fancy. In perfect health a chance moment of warm recollection will bring from this source the once familiar face transiently, but how distinctly, before the heart.

In its morbid state the beings it projects before us are for the most part strangers; just as the personages we meet in our dreams are exceptionally only our living and present acquaintance.

The most instructive case of sensorial illusions on record, as containing the largest illustration of their phenomena, is that of Nicolai, the bookseller of Berlin. The narrative was read before the academy of sciences at Berlin in 1799. Its substance runs thus; — Nicolai had met with some family troubles, which much disturbed him. Then on the first of January 1791, there stood before him at the distance of ten paces the ghost of his eldest son. He pointed at it directing his wife to look. She saw it not, and tried to convince Nicolai that it was an illusion. In a quarter of an hour it vanished. In the afternoon, at four o'clock, it came again. Nicolai was alone. He went to his wife's room, the ghost followed him. About six other apparitions joined the first, and they walked about among each other. After some days the apparition of his son stayed away. But its place was filled with the figures of a number of persons, some known, some unknown to Nicolai — some of dead, others of living persons. The known ones represented distant acquaintances only. The figures of none of Nicolai's habitual friends were there. The appearances were almost always human; occasionally a man on horseback, and birds, and dogs, would present themselves. The apparitions came mostly after dinner, at the commencement of digestion. They were just like real persons; the colouring a thought fainter. The apparitions were equally distinct whether Nicolai was alone or in society, in the dark as by day, in his own house or in those of others; but in the latter case they were less frequent, and they very seldom made their appearance in the streets. During the first eight days they seemed to take very little notice of one another, but walked about like people at a fair, only here and there communing with each other. They took no notice of Nicolai, or of the remarks he addressed regarding them to his wife and physician. No effort of his would dismiss them or bring an absent one back. When he shut his eyes, they sometimes disappeared, sometimes remained; when he opened his eyes, they were there as before. After a week they became more numerous and began to converse. They conversed with one another first, and then addressed him. Their remarks were short and unconnected, but sensible and civil. His acquaintances inquired after his health and expressed sympathy with him, and spoke in terms comforting him. The apparitions were most conversible when he was alone; nevertheless they mingled in the conversation when others were by, and their voices had the same sound as those of real persons. The illusion went on thus from the 24th of February to the 20th of April, so that Nicolai, who was in good bodily health, had time to become tranquillized about them, and to observe them at his ease. At last they rather amused him. Then the Doctors thought of an efficient plan of treatment. They prescribed leeches; and then followed the "denouement" of this interesting representation. The apparitions became pale and vanished. On the 20th of April at the time of applying the leeches, Nicolai's room was full of figures moving about among each other. They first began to have a less lively motion; shortly afterwards their colours became paler, in another half hour paler still, though the forms still remained. About seven o'clock in the evening the figures had become colourless, and they moved scarcely at all, but their outline was still tolerably perfect. Gradually that became less and less defined; at last they disappeared, breaking into air, fragments only remaining, which at last all vanished. By eight o'clock all were gone, and Nicolai subsequently saw no more of them.

In general, as in Nicolai's case, the sight is the sense at first and alone affected. Illusions of the hearing, if they occur, follow later. In some most extraordinary cases I have observed that the touch has likewise participated on the affection. The following is an instance.

Herr von Baczko, already subject to visual hallucinations, of a diseased nervous system, his right side weak with palsy, his right eye blind and the vision of the left imperfect, was engaged one evening shortly after the battle of Jena, as he tells in his autobiography, in translating a pamphlet into Polish, when he felt a poke in his loins.

He looked round, and found that it proceeded from a negro or Aegyptian boy, seemingly about twelve years of age. Altho' he was persuaded the whole was an illusion, he thought it best to knock the apparition down, when he felt that it offered a sensible resistance. The negro then attacked him on the other side and gave his left arm a particularly disagreeable twist, when Baczko again pushed him off. The negro continued to visit him constantly during four months, preserving the same appearance, and remaining tangible, then he came seldomer; and finally appearing as a brown coloured apparition with an owl's head, he took his leave.

Sensorial illusions technically speaking are not mental delusions; or they become so only when they are believed to be realities. So sensorial illusions are not insanity; neither do they menace that disorder; they are not its customary precursors. Nevertheless they may accompany the first outbreak of madness; and they occur much more frequently in lunatics than in persons of sound mind. In insanity they are firmly believed in by the patient, whose delusions they may either suggest or be shaped by. In insanity illusions of the hearing often occur alone, which is extremely rare in sane people.

The objects of visual illusions are commonly men and women; but animals and even inanimate objects sometimes constitute them. A lady whose sight was failing her had long visions every day of rows of buildings, houses and parks, and such like. The subjects of visual illusions are generally perfectly trivial; like the events of a common dream. But, tho' susceptible of change, their custom is to recur with much the same character daily. One patient could at will summon the apparition of an acquaintance to join the rest; but once there he could not get rid of him.

Sometimes it happens that sensorial illusions are in accordance with a congenial train of thought; — for instance with peculiar impressions referring to religion. They are then very liable to be construed by the patient into realities, and to materially influence his conversation and conduct. He remains no doubt strictly sane in the midst of these delusions. But he is apt not to be thought so. Or to use a figure, the worlds opinion of such a person becomes a polar force; and society is divided into his admiring followers, and those who think him a lunatic. Such was and remains the fate of Schwedenborg.

Schwedenborg, the son of a swedish clergyman of the name of Schwedberg, ennobled as Schwedenborg, was up to the year 1743, which was the fifty-fourth of his age, an ordinary man of the world, distinguished only in literature, having written many volumes on Philosophy and science, and being professor in the mineralogical school, where he was much respected. On a sudden, in the year 1743, he believed himself to have got into a commerce with the world of spirits; which so fully took possession of his thoughts, that he not only published their revelations, but was in the habit of detailing their daily chat with him. Thus he says, "I had a conversation the other day on that very point with the apostle Paul;" or with Luther, or some other dead person. Schwedenborg continued to be in what he believed to be constant communion with spirits till his death, in 1772. He was without doubt in the fullest degree convinced of the reality of his spiritual commerce. So in a letter to the Wurtemburg Prelate, Oetinger, dated November 11, 1766, he uses the following words; — "If I have spoken with the apostles? To this I answer, I conversed with St. Paul during a whole year, particularly with reference to the text, Romans III. 28. I have three times conversed with St. John, once with Moses, and a hundred times with Luther, who allowed that it was against the warning of an angel that he professed "fidem solam" and that he stood alone upon the separation from the Pope. With angels, finally, have I these twenty years conversed, and converse daily."

Of the angels he says "they have human forms, the appearance of men, as I have a thousand times seen; for I have spoken with them as a man with other men, often with several together, and I have seen nothing in the least to distinguish them from other men." They had in fact exactly the same appearance as Nicolai's visitors. "Lest any one should call this an illusion or imaginary perception, it is to be understood that I am accustomed to see them, when myself perfectly wide awake, and in full exercize of my observation. The speech of an angel or of a spirit sounds like, and as loud as that of a man; but it is not heard by the bystanders. The reason is that *the speech of an angel or a spirit finds entrance first into a man's thoughts, and reaches his organs of hearing from within.*" A wonderful instance this last reason, how it is possible *cum ratione insanire;* he analyzes the illusion perfectly, even when he is most deceived by it.

"The angels who converse with men speak not in their own language, but in the language of the country; and likewise in other languages which are known to a man, not in languages which he does not understand." Schwedenborg here interrupted the angels, and to explain the matter, observed, that they most likely appeared to speak his mother-tongue, *because, in fact,* it was not they who spoke, but himself after their suggestions. The angels would not allow this, and went away at the close of the conversation unpersuaded.

The following fiction is very fine. "When approaching, the angels often appear like a ball of light; and they travel in companies so grouped together — they are allowed so to unite by the Lord — that they may act as one being, and share each other's ideas and knowledge; and in this form they bound through the universe, from planet to planet."

A still more interesting example of the influence of sensorial illusions on human conduct is furnished by the touching history of Joan of Arc.

"It is now seven years ago," so spoke before her judges the simple but high minded maiden, — "It was a summer day, towards the middle hour; I was about thirteen years old, and was in my fathers garden, — that I heard for the first time on my right hand, towards the church, a voice, and there stood a figure in a bright radiance before my eyes. It had the appearance and look of a right good and virtuous man, bore wings, was surrounded with light on all sides and by the angels of Heaven. It was the archangel Michael. The voice seemed to me to command respect; but I was yet a child, and was frightened at the figure, and doubted very much whether it were the archangel. I saw him and the angels as distinctly before my eyes as I now see you, my judges." With words of encouragement the archangel announced to her, that God had taken pity upon France, and that she must hasten to the assistance of the King. At the same time he promised her that St. Catherine and St. Margaret would shortly visit her: he told her that she should do what they commanded her; because they were sent by God to guide and conduct her. "Upon this," continued Joan, "St. Catherine and St. Margaret appeared to me, as the archangel had foretold. They ordered me to get ready to go to Robert de Beaudricourt, the kings captain. He would several time refuse me, but at last would consent, and give me people, who would conduct me to the king. Then should I raise the siege of Orleans. I replied to them, that I was a poor child, who understood nothing about riding on horseback and making war. They said I should carry my banner with courage; God would help me, and win back for my king his entire kingdom. As soon as I knew," continued Joan, "that I was to proceed on this errand, I avoided as much as I could, taking part in the sports and amusements of my young companions." — "So have the saints conducted me during seven years, and have given me support and assistance in all my need and labours; and now at present" said she to her judges, "no day goes by, but they come to see me." — "I seldom see the saints that they are not surrounded with a halo of light; they wear rich and precious crowns, as it is reasonable they should. I see them always under the same forms, and have never found in their discourse any discrepancies. I know how to distinguish one from the other, and distinguish them as well by the sound of their voices as by their salutation. They come often without my calling upon them. But when they do not come, I pray to the Lord that he will send them to me; and never have I needed them but they have visited me."

Such is part of the defence of the heroic Joan of Arc, who was taken prisoner by the Duke of Burgundy on the 23 of May 1430 — sold by him for a large sum to the English, and by them put on her trial as a heretic, idolatress, and magician — condemned and finally burned alive the 30th of May 1431!

Her innocence, simplicity and courage incense one sadly against her judges; but it is likely there were at the time many good and sensible persons who approved of her sentence and never suspected its cruelty and injustice. Making allowance for the ignorance and barbarity of the age her treatment was perhaps not worse than that of Abdel Kader now. Her visions; — they were palpably the productions of her own fancy, the figures of saints and angels which she had seen in missals projected before her mental sight; and their cause; — the instinctive workings, unknown to herself, of her young high couraged and enthusiastic heart, shaping its suggestions into holy prophecyings; the leading facts of which her resolute will realized while their actual discrepancies with subsequent events, she pardonably forgot.

I will present yet another and less pleasing picture, where the subject of sensorial illusions was of infirm mind, and they struck upon the insane cord, and reason jangled harshly out of tune. It would be a curious question whether such a sensorial illusion, as overthrew the young seer's judgment in the following case, could have occurred to a mind previously sane; — whether for instance it could have occurred to Schwedenborg, and in that event how he would have dealt with it.

Arnold (a german writer) relates in his history of the church and of heresy, how there was a young man in Königsberg, well educated, the natural son of a priest, who had the impression that he was met near a crucifix on the wayside by seven angels, who revealed to him that he was to represent God the Father on earth, to drive all evil out of the world, etc. The poor fellow after pondering upon this illusion a long time issued a circular beginning thus; —

"We, John Albrecht, Adelgreif, Syrdos, Amata, Kanemata, Kilkis, Mataldis, Schmalkilimundis, Sabrandis, Elioris, Hyperarch-High-priest and Emperor, Prince of peace of the whole world, Hyperarch-King of the holy kingdom of Heaven, judge of the living and of the dead, God and Father, in whose divinity Christ will come on the last day to judge the world, Lord of all Lords, King of all Kings, etc. —

He was thereupon thrown into prison at Königsberg; where every means were used by the clergy to reclaim him from these blasphemous and heretical notions. To all their entreaties, however, he listened only with a smile of pity, "— that they should think of reclaiming God the Father." He was then put to the torture, and as what he endured made no alteration in his convictions, he was condemned to have his tongue torn out with red-hot-tongs, to be cut in four quarters, and then burned under the gallows. He wept bitterly, not at his own fate, but that they should pronounce such a sentence on the Deity. The executioner was touched with pity, and implored him to make a final recantation. But he persisted that he was God the Father, whether they pulled his tongue out by the roots or not; and so he was executed!

From the preceding forcible illustrations of the working of sensorial illusions on individual minds, it is to descend a little in interest to trace their ministry in giving rise to the ricketty forms of popular superstition. However, the material may be the same, whether it be cast for the commemoration of a striking event, or coined for vulgar currency. And here is a piece of the latter description, with the recommendation of being at least fresh from the mint and spic and span, — an instance of superstition, surviving in England in the middle of the nineteenth century.

A young gentleman, who has recently left Oxford, told me that he was one evening at a supper-party in college, when they were joined by a common friend on his return from hunting. They expected him, but were struck with his appearance. He was pale and agitated. On questioning him they learned the cause. During the latter part of his ride home he had been accompanied by a horseman, who kept exact pace with him; the rider and horse being close fac-similes of himself and the steed he rode, even to the copy of a new-fangled bit which he sported that day for the first time. He had in fact seen his "double" or "Fetch;" and it had shaken his nerves pretty considerably. His friends advised him to consult the college-tutor, who failed not to give him some good advice and hoped the warning would not be thrown away. My informant, who thought the whole matter very serious and was inclined to believe the unearthly visit to have been no idle one, added that it had made the ghost-seer for the time at least a wiser and better man.

Such a visionary duplicate of oneself, one's fetch, is a not unfrequent form of sensorial illusion. In more ignorant days the appearance of a fetch excited much apprehension. It was supposed to menace death or serious calamity to its original. Properly viewed, unless it proceed from hard work and overstrained thought (from which you can desist) it indicates something wrong in your physical health, and its warning goes no further than to consult a doctor, to learn "what rhubarb, senna, or what purgative drug, will drive the spectre hence." The efficiency of such means was shewn in the case of Nicolai. Yet in his case, I may remark, the originating cause of the attack had been anxiety about the very son, whose apparition was the first of the throng to visit him. Had the illusion continued limited to the figure of the son, it would have been more questionable what art could do towards dismissing it. At all events in such a case the first thing is to remove the perilous stuff that weighs upon the mind. So the personage whose words I have been using was doubtless right in his own case to "throw physic to the dogs."

In the tragedy of Macbeth sensorial illusions are made to play their part with curious physiological correctness. The mind of Macbeth is worn by the conflict between ambition and duty; at last his better resolves give way; and his excited fancy projects before him the fetch of his own dagger, which marshals him the way that he shall go. The spectator is thus artistically prepared for the further working of the same infirmity in the apparition of Banquo, which unseen by his guests is visible only to the conscience-stricken murderer. With a scientific precision, no less admirable, the partner of his guilt, *a woman,* is made to have attacks of trance, *(to which women are more liable than men)* caused by her disturbed mind; and in her trance the exact physiological character of one form of that disorder is pourtrayed, — *she enacts a dream,* which is the essence of somnambulism.

One almost doubts whether Shakespeare was aware

of the philosophic truth displayed in these masterstrokes of his own art. The apparitions conjured up in the witch-scenes of the same play, and the ghost in Hamlet, are moulded on the pattern of vulgar superstition. He employs indifferently the baser metal and the truthful inspirations of his own genius, — realizing Shelley's strange figure of

"a poet hidden
'In the light of thought."

As they say the sun is himself dark as a planet, and his atmosphere alone the source of light, through the gaps in which his common earth is seen. I am tempted, but it would be idle and I refrain, to quote an expression or two, or a passage, from Shakespeare, exemplifying his wonderful turn for approximating to truths of which he must have been ignorant; — where lines of admired and unaccountable beauty have unexpectedly acquired lucidity and appositeness through modern science. While, to make a quaint comparison, his great contemporary Bacon employed the lamp of his imagination to illuminate the paths to the discovery of truth, Shakespeare would with random intuition seize on the undiscovered truths themselves and use them to vivify the conceptions of his fancy.

Let me now turn to explain a ghost of a more positive description, the church-yard ghost. The ghost will perhaps exclaim against so trivial a title, and one unjust in reference to old superstition; but it will be seen he deserves no better. In popular story he had a higher office; his duty was to watch the body, over which church-rites had not been performed, that had been rudely inearthed after violent death. As thus.

There was a cottage in a village I could name, to which a bad report attached; more than one who had slept in it had seen at midnight the radiant apparition of a little child, standing on the hearth-stone. At length suspicion was awakened. The hearth-stone was raised, and there were found buried beneath it the remains of an infant. A story was now divulged how the last tenant and a female of the village had abruptly quitted the neighbourhood. The ghost was real and significant enough.

But here is a still better instance from a trustworthy german work P. Kieffer's Archives. The narrative was communicated by Herr Ehrman of Strasburg, son in law of the well known writer Pfeffel, from whom he received it.

The ghost-seer was a young candidate for orders, eighteen years of age, of the name of Billing. He was known to have very excitable nerves, had already experienced sensorial illusions, and was particularly sensitive to the presence of human remains, which made him tremble and shudder in all his limbs. Pfeffel, being blind, was accustomed to take the arm of this young man, and they walked thus together in Pfeffel's garden, near Colmar. At one spot in the garden Pfeffel remarked that his companion's arm gave a sudden start, as if he had received an electric shock. Being asked what was the matter, Belling replied, "nothing." But on their going over the same spot again, the same effect recurred. The young man being pressed to explain the cause of his disturbance, avowed that it arose from a peculiar sensation, which he always experienced when in the vicinity of human remains; that it was his impression a human body must be interred there; but that if Pfeffel would return with him at night, he should be able to speak with greater confidence. Accordingly they went together to the garden when it was dark, and as they approached the spot Billing observed a faint light over it. At ten paces from it he stopped, and would go no farther; for he saw hovering over it, or self supported in the air, its feet only a few inches from the ground, a luminous female figure, nearly five feet high, with the right arm folded on her breast, the left hanging by her side. When Pfeffel himself stepped forward and placed himself about where the figure appeared to be, Billing said it was now on his right hand, now on his left, now behind, now before him. When Pfeffel cut the air with his stick, it seemed as if it went through and divided a light flame, which then united again. The visit, repeated the next night, in company with some of Pfeffel's relatives, gave the same result. They did not see any thing. Pfeffel then unknown to the ghost-seer, had the ground dug up, when there was found at some depth, beneath a layer of quicklime, a human body in progress of decomposition. The remains were removed and the earth carefully replaced. Three days afterwards Billing, from whom this whole proceeding had been kept concealed, was again led to the spot by Pfeffel. He walked over it now without experiencing any unusual impression whatever.

The explanation of this mysterious phenomenon has been, but recently, arrived at. The discoveries of von Reichenbach, of which I gave a sketch in the first letter, announce the principle on which it depends. Among these discoveries is the fact that the od force makes itself visible as a dim light or waving flame to highly sensitive subjects. Such persons in the dark see flames issuing from the poles of magnets and crystals. von Reichenbach eventually discovered that the od force is distributed universally altho' in varying quantities. But among the causes, which excite its evolution one of the most active is chemical decomposition. Then happening to remember Pfeffel's ghost-story it occurred to von

Reichenbach, that what Billing had seen, was possibly od light. To test the soundness of this conjecture, Miss Reichel, a very sensitive subject, was taken at night to an extensive burying ground near Vienna, where interments take place daily, and there are many thousand graves. The result did not disappoint von Reichenbach's expectations. Whither-so-ever Miss Reichel turned her eyes, she saw masses of flame. This appearance manifested itself most about recent graves. About very old ones it was not visible. She described the appearance as resembling less bright flame than fiery vapour, something between fog and flame. In several instances the light extended four feet in height above the ground. When Miss Reichel placed her hand on it, it seemed to her involved in a cloud of fire. When she stood in it, it came up to her throat. She expressed no alarm being accustomed to the appearance.

The mystery has thus been entirely solved. For it is evident that the spectral character of the luminous apparition in the two instances which I have narrated had been supplied by the seers themselves. So the superstition has vanished; but as usual it veiled a truth.

Letter IV
REAL GHOSTS

The worst of a true ghost, is that to be sure of his genuineness, that is, of his veracity, one must wait the event. He is distinguished by no sensible and positive characteristics from the commoner herd. There is nothing in his outward appearance to raise him in your opinion above a fetch. But even this fact is not barren. His dress, — it is in the ordinary mode of the time, in nothing overdone; — to be dressed thus does credit to his taste, as to be dressed at all evinces his sense of propriety; — but alas, the same elements convict him of unreality. Whence come that aerial coat and waistcoat, whence those visionary trowsers? alas, they can only have issued from the wardrobe in the seer's fancy. And like his dress, the wearer is imaginary, a mere sensorial illusion, without a shadow of externality; he is not more substantial than a dream.

But dreams have differences of quality no less than ghosts. All do not come through the ivory gate. Some are real, true, and significant enough. See, there glides one skulking assassinlike into the shade, he not long since killed his man; "Hilloa, ill-favoured dream, come hither and give an account of yourself." (enter dream.)

A scottish gentleman and his wife were travelling four or five years ago in Switzerland. There travelled with them a third party, an intimate friend, a lady, who some time before had been the object of a deep attachment on the part of a foreigner, a Frenchman. Well, she would have nothing to say to him on the topic uppermost in his mind, but she gave him a good deal of serious advice, which she probably thought he wanted; and she ultimately promoted, or was a cognizant party to his union with a lady, whom she likewise knew. The so-married couple were now in America. And the lady, occasionally heard from them, and had every reason to believe they were both in perfect health. One morning on their meeting at breakfast, she told her companions, that she had had a very impressive dream the night before, which had recurred twice. The scene was a room in which lay a coffin; near to it stood her ex-lover in a luminous transfigured, resplendent state; his wife was by looking much as usual. The dream had caused the lady some misgivings; but her companions exhorted her to view it as a trick of her fancy, and she was half persuaded so to do. The dream, however, was right notwithstanding. In process of time letters arrived announcing the death after a short illness of the french gentleman, within the twenty fours in which the vision appeared. (sensation; applause, followed by cries of shame; the dream hurrying away is hurt by the horn of the gate.)

It would be difficult to persuade the lady who dreamed this dream, that there was no connexion between it and the event it fore-shadowed in her mind beyond the accidental coincidence of time. Nevertheless to this conclusion an indifferent auditor would probably come; and upon the following reasoning. We sometimes dream of the death of an absent friend, when he is alive and in health, just as we sometimes dream that long lost friends are alive. And it is quite possible, — nay likely to occur in the chapter of accidents, — nay certain to turn up now and then among the dreams of millions during centuries, — that a fortuitous dream seemingly referring to the fact should be coincident in point of time with the death of a distant friend. To explain one such case we need look no further than to the operation of chance. Why then ever seek another principle?

Let us examine a parallel ghost-story. A gentleman has a relative in India, of good constitution, in the civil service, prosperous. He has no cause for anxiety and entertains none, respecting his relative. But one day he sees his ghost. In due course letters arrive mentioning the occurrence of his relative's death on that day. The case is more remarkable than the last. For the ghostseer never in his life *but that once* experienced a sensorial illusion. Still it is evidently possible that the two events were through chance alone coincident in time. And if in this case, why not in another?

Then let me adduce a stranger instance. A late general Wynyard, and the late general Sir John Sherbroke, when young men, were serving in Canada. One day, — it was daylight — Mr. Wynyard and Mr. Sherbroke both saw pass through the room where they sat a figure, which Mr. Wynyard recognized as a brother then far away. One of the two walked to the door, and looked out upon the landing place; but the stranger was not there, and a servant who was in the stairs had seen nobody pass out. In time news arrived that Mr. Wynyard's brother had died about the time of the visit of the apparition.

I have had opportunities of inquiring of two near relations of this general Wynyard upon what evidence the above story rests. They told me that they had each heard it from his own mouth. More recently, a gentleman, whose accuracy of recollection exceeds that of most people, has told me, that he had heard the late Sir John Sherbroke, the other party in the ghost story, tell it much in the same way at a dinner-table.

One does not feel as comfortably satisfied that the complicated coincidences in this tale admit of being referred to chance. The odds are enormous against two persons, young men in perfect health, neither of whom before or after this event experienced a sensorial illusion, being the subjects at the same moment of one, their common and only one, which concurred in point of time with an event that it foreshadowed, — unless there were some real connexion between the event and the double apparition. And we feel a nascent inclination to inquire, whether — in case such instances as the present occasionally turn up, and instances like the two before narrated become, when looked for, startlingly multiplied, —

there exist any known mental or physical principle, by the help of which they may be explained into natural phenomena.

The more we look after facts of the above nature, the more urgent becomes the want of such an explanation. In every family circle, in every party of men accidentally brought together, you will be sure to hear, if the conservation fall on ghosts and dreams, one or more instances, which the narrators represent as well authenticated, of intimations of the deaths of absent persons conveyed to friends either through an apparition, or a dream, or an equivalent unaccountable presentiment. A gentleman, himself of distinguished ability, told me that when he was an undergraduate at Cambridge, he was secretary to a ghost-society formed in sportive earnest by some of the cleverest young men of one of the best modern periods of the university. The result of their labours was the collection of about a dozen stories of the above description resting upon good evidence.

Then there transpire occasionally cases with more curious features still. Not only is the general intimation of an event given, but minute particulars attending it, are figured in the dream or communicated by the ghost. Such tales have sometimes figured in courts of justice. Here is one out of last week's newspaper.

"In a Durham paper of last week, there was an account of the disappearance of Mr. Smith, gardener to Sir Clifford Constable, who it was supposed had fallen into the river Tees, his hat and stick having been found near the water-side. From that time up to Friday last the river had been dragged every day; but every effort so made to find the body proved ineffectual. On the night of Thursday, however, a person named Awde, residing at little Newsham, a small village about four miles from Wycliffe, dreamt that Smith was laid under the ledge of a certain rock, about three hundred yards below Whorlton-bridge, and *that his right arm was broken.* Awde got up early on Friday, and his dream had such an effect upon him that he determined to go and search the river. He accordingly started off for that purpose, without mentioning the matter, being afraid that he would be laughed at by his neighbours. Nevertheless, on his arriving at the boat-house he disclosed his object on the man asking him for what purpose he required the boat. He rowed to the spot he had seen in his dream; and there, strange to say, upon the very first trial that he made with his boat-hook, he pulled up the body of the unfortunate man, with his right arm actually broken." (Herald, December 1848.)

Reviewing all that I have advanced it appears to me that there are two desiderata which pressingly require to be now supplied. First, some one should take the pains of authenticating at the time and putting on permanent record stories like the above to be at the service of future speculators. But secondly so numerous and well attested are those already current, that the production into light of some principle, by which they may be shewn to be natural events, is now peremptorily called for.

To lead to the supply of the second desideratum, I proceed to mention a psychical phenomenon, which from time to time occurred to the late historian and novelist, Heinrich Zschokke. It is described by him in a sort of autobiography, entitled "Selbstschau," which he published a few years ago. It is only last year that Zschokke died having attained a good old age. Early brought into public life in the troubles of Switzerland, and afterwards maintaining his place in public consideration by his numerous writings, he was personally widely known; he was universally esteemed a man of strict veracity and integrity. He writes thus of himself.

"If the reception of so many visitors was sometimes troublesome, it repaid itself occasionally either by making me acquainted with remarkable personages, or by bringing out a wonderful sort of seer-gift, which I called my inward vision, and which has always remained an enigma to me. I am almost afraid to say a word upon this subject, not for fear of the imputation of being superstitious, but lest I should encourage that disposition in others; and yet it forms a contribution to psychology. So to confess.

"It is acknowledged that the judgment, which we form of strangers on first meeting them, is frequently more correct than that, which we adopt upon a longer acquaintance with them. The first impression, which through an instinct of the soul attracts one towards, or repels one from another, becomes after a time more dim, and is weakened, either through his appearing other than at first, or through our becoming accustomed to him. People speak too in reference to such cases of involuntary sympathies and aversions, and attach a special certainty to such manifestations in children, in whom knowledge of mankind by experience is wanting. Others again are incredulous, and attribute all to physiognomical skill. But of myself.

"It has happened to me occasionally, at the first meeting with a total stranger, when I have been listening in silence to his conversation, that his past life, up to the present moment, with many minute circumstances belonging to one or other particular scene in it, has come across me like a dream, but distinctly, entirely involuntarily and unsought, occupying in duration a few minutes. During this period I am usually so plunged into the representation of the strangers life, that at last I neither continue to see distinctly his face, on which I was idly speculating, nor to hear intelligently his voice, which at first I was using as a commentary to the text of his physiognomy. For a long time I was disposed to consider these fleeting visions as a trick of the fancy; the more so that my dream-vision displayed to me the dress and movements of the actors, the appearance of the room, the furniture and other accidents of the scene. Till on one occasion, in a gamesome mood, I narrated to my family the secret history of a sempstress, who had just before quitted the room. I had never seen the person before. Nevertheless the hearers were astonished, and laughed, and would not be persuaded but that I had a previous acquaintance with the former life of the person, in as much as what I had stated was perfectly true. I was not less astonished to find that my dream-vision agreed with reality. I then gave more attention to the subject, and as often as propriety allowed of it, I related to those, whose lives had so past before me, the substance of my dream-vision, to obtain from them its contradiction or confirmation. On every occasion its confirmation followed, not without amazement on the part of those who gave it.

"Least of all could I myself give faith to these conjuring tricks of my mind. Every time that I described to any one my dream-vision respecting him, I confidently expected him to answer, it was not so. A secret thrill always came over me, when the listener replied, "it happened as you say," or when before he spoke, his astonishment betrayed that I was not wrong. Instead of recording many instances, I will give one, which at the time made a strong impression upon me. —

"On a fair-day, I went into the town of Waldshut, accompanied by two young foresters who are still alive. It was evening, and tired with our walk we went into an inn called the Vine. We took our supper with a numerous company at the public table; when it happened that they made themselves merry over the peculiarities and simplicity of the Swiss, in connexion with the belief in Mesmerism, Lavater's physiognomical system, and the like. One of my companions, whose national pride was touched by their raillery, begged me to make some reply, particularly in answer to a young man of superior appearance, who sat opposite and had indulged in unrestrained ridicule. It happened that the events of this very person's life had just previously passed before my mind. I turned to him with the question, whether he would reply to me with truth and candour, if I narrated to him the most secret passages of his history, he being as little known to me as I to him. That would, I suggested, go something beyond Lavater's physiognomical skill. He promised, if I told the truth, to admit it openly. Then I narrated the events with which my dream-vision had furnished me, and the table learnt the history of the young tradesman's life, of his school years, his peccadilloes, and finally of a little act of roguery committed by him on the strong box of his employer. I described the uninhabited room with its white walls, where to the right of the brown door, there had stood upon the table the small black moneychest, etc. A dead silence reigned in the company during this recital, interrupted only when I occasionally asked if I spoke the truth. The man, much struck, admitted the correctness of each circumstance, — even which I could not expect, of the last. Touched with his frankness I reached my hand to him across the table and closed my narrative. He asked my name, which I gave him. We sat up late in the night conversing. He may be alive yet.

"Now I can well imagine how a lively imagination could picture, romance-fashion, from the obvious character of a person, how he would conduct himself under given circumstances. But whence came to me the involuntary knowledge of accessory details, which were without any sort of interest, and respected people who for the most part were utterly indifferent to me, with whom I neither had, nor wished to have, the slightest association? Or was it on each case mere coincidence? Or had the listener, to whom I described his history, each time other images in his mind than the accessory ones of my story, but, in surprize at the essential resemblance of my story to the truth, lost sight of the points of difference? Yet I have in consideration of this possible source of error, several times taken pains to describe the most trivial circumstances that my dream-vision has shewn me.

"Not another word about this strange seer-gift, — which I can aver was of no use to me in a single instance, which manifested itself occasionally only, and quite independently of any volition, and often in relation to persons, in whose history I took not the slightest interest. Nor am I the only one in possession of this faculty. In a journey with two of my sons, I fell in with an old Tyrolese, who travelled about selling lemons and oranges, at the Inn at Unterhauerstein in one of the Jura passes. He fixed his eyes for some time upon me, joined in our conversation, observed that though I did not know him he knew me, and began to describe my acts and deeds to the no little amusement of the peasants and astonishment of my children, whom it interested to learn that another possessed the same gift as their father. How the old lemon-merchant acquired his knowledge, he was not able to explain to himself nor to me. But he seemed to attach great importance to his hidden wisdom."

In the newness of such knowledge it is worth-while to note separately each of the particulars, which attended the manifestation of this strange mental faculty, with his account of which Zschokke has enriched psychology.

1. Then, after the power of looking through the entire recollections of another, through some other channel than ordinary inquiry and observation, — and as it seemed *directly*, — we may note.

2. The rapidity, minuteness, and precision, which characterized the act of inspection.

3. The feeling attending it of becoming absent or lost to what was going on around.

4. Its involuntariness and unexpectedness.

5. Its being practicable on some only; and

6. those, strangers and at their first interview with the seer.

At present I shall avail myself of the first broad fact alone, — remarking however of the conditions observed in it, that they clearly indicate the existence of a law on which the phenomenon depended. And I shall assume it to be proved by the above crucial instance, that the mind, or soul, of one human being can be brought in the natural course of things, and under physiological laws hereafter to be determined, into immediate relation with the mind of another living person.

If this principle be admitted, it is adequate to explain all the puzzling phenomena of real ghosts and of true dreams. For example the ghostly and intersomnial communications, with which we have as yet dealt, have been announcements of the deaths of absent parties. Suppose our new principle brought into play; — the soul of the dying person is to be supposed to have come into direct communication with the mind of his friend, with the effect of suggesting his present condition. If the seer be dreaming, the suggestion shapes a corresponding dream; if he be awake it originates a sensorial illusion. To speak figuratively, *merely figuratively*, in reference to the circulation of this partial mental obituary, I will suppose that the death of a human being throws a sort of gleam through the spiritual world, which may now and then touch with light some fittingly disposed object; or even two simultaneously, if chance have placed them in the right relation; — as the twin-spires of a cathedral may be momentarily illuminated by some far-off flash, which does not break the gloom upon the roofs below.

The same principle is applicable to the explanation of the vampyr-visit. The soul of the buried man is to be supposed to be brought into communication with his friend's mind. Thence follows, as a sensorial illusion, the apparition of the buried man. Perhaps the visit may have been an instinctive effort to draw the attention of his friend to his living grave. I beg to suggest that it would not be an act of superstition *now*, but of ordinary humane precaution, if one dreamed pertinaciously of a recently buried acquaintance, or saw his ghost, to take immediate steps to have the state of the body ascertained.

It is not my intention in the present letter to push the application of this principle further. With slight modifications it might be brought to explain several other wonderful stories, which one usually neglects just from not seeing how to explain them. The faculty of second-sight is dropping fast out of recollection. If it ever existed, it seems to be disappearing now. But it is difficult, one has heard so many instances of the correctness of its warnings and anticipations, not to believe that it once really manifested itself.

A much respected scottish lady, not unknown in literature, told me very recently, how a friend of her mother, whom she perfectly remembered, had been compelled to believe in second-sight through its occurrence in one of her servants. She had a cook, who was a continual annoyance to her through her possession of this gift. On one occasion when the lady expected some friends, she learned a short time before they were to arrive, that the culinary preparations she had ordered to honor them had not been made. Upon her remonstrating with the offending cook, the latter simply but doggedly assured her, that come they would not; that she knew it of a certainty; and true enough they did not come. Some accident had occurred to prevent their visit. The same person frequently knew beforehand what her mistress's plans were, and was as inconvenient in her kitchen as a calculating prodigy in a counting-house. Things went perfectly right, but the manner was irregular and provoking; so her mistress turned her away. Supposing this story true, the phenomena look just a modification of Zschokke's seer-gift.

A number of incidents there are turning up for the most part on trivial occasions, which we put aside for fear of being thought superstitious, because as yet a natural solution is not at hand for them. Sympathy in general, the spread of panic fears, the simultaneous occurrence of the same thoughts to two persons, the intuitive knowledge of mankind possessed by some, the magnetic fascination of others, may eventually be found to have to do with a special and unsuspected cause. Among anecdotes of no great conclusiveness that I have heard narrated of this sort, I will cite two, of Lord Nelson, told by the late Sir J. Hardy to the late Admiral the hon^{ble} G. Dundas, from whom I heard them. The first was mentioned to exemplify Nelson's quick insight into character. Captain Hardy was present as Nelson gave directions to the commander of a frigate, to make sail with all speed — to proceed to certain points, where he was likely to fall in with the french fleet, — having seen the french to go to a certain harbour and there await Lord Nelson's coming. After the commander had left the cabin, Nelson said to Hardy, "He will go to the west Indies, he will see the

French; he will go to the harbour I have directed him to; but he will not wait for me; he will sail for England." The commander did so. Shortly before the battle of Trafalgar an English frigate was in advance looking out for the enemy; her place in the offing was hardly discernible. Of a sudden Nelson said to Hardy, with whom he was pacing the deck of the Victory; — "The celeste," (or whatever the frigate's name was) "the celeste sees the French." Hardy had nothing to say on the matter. "She sees the French; she'll fire a gun." Within a little the boom of the signal-gun was heard.

I am not sure that my new principle will be a general favorite. It will be said that the cases, in which I suppose it manifested, are of too trivial a nature to justify so novel an hypothesis. My answer is, the cases are few and trivial only because the subject has not been attended to. For how many centuries were the laws of electricity preindicated by the single fact, that a piece of amber when rubbed would attract light bodies? The school of physiological materialists will of course be opposed to it. They hold that the mind is but a function or product of the brain, and cannot therefore consistently admit its separate action. But their fundamental tenet is unsound, even upon considering the analogies of matter alone.

What is meant by a product? in what does production consist? Let us look for instances; a metal is produced from an ore; — alkohol is produced from saccharine matter; — the bones and sinews of an animal are produced from its food. Production in the strict sense of the word means the conversion of one substance into another weight for weight, agreeably with, or under, mechanicial, chemical, and vital laws. If mind be the product of the brain it must be the conversion of so much brain weight for weight into thought and feeling, which is an absurdity.

It is indeed true that with the manifestation of each thought or feeling a corresponding decomposition of the brain takes place. But it is equally true that in a Voltaic battery in action, each movement of electric force developed there is attended with a waste of the metal-plates which help to form it. But that waste is not converted into electric fluid. The exact quantity of pure copper which disappears may be detected in the form of sulphate of copper. The electricity was *not produced; it was only set in motion* by the chemical decomposition. Here is the true material analogy of the relation of the brain to the mind. Mind, like electricity, is an imponderable force pervading the universe: and there happen to be known to us certain material arrangements, through which each may be influenced. We cannot indeed pursue the analogy beyond this step. Consciousness and electricity have nothing further in common. Their further relations to the dissimilar material arrangements, through which they may be excited or disturbed, are subjects of totally distinct studies, and resolvable into laws which have no affinity and admit of no comparison.

It is singular how early in the history of mankind the belief in the separate existence of the soul developed itself as an instinct of our nature.

Timarchus, who was curious on the subject of the demon of Socrates, went to the cave of Trophonius to consult the oracle about it. There, having for a short time inhaled the mephitic vapor, he felt as if he had received a sudden blow in the head, and sank down insensible. Then his head appeared to him to open and to give issue to his soul into the other world; and an imaginary being seemed to inform him, that "the part of the soul engaged in the body, entrammelled in its organization, is the soul as ordinarily understood; but that there is another part or province of the soul which is the daimon. This has a certain control over the bodily soul, and among other offices constitutes conscience:" — "In three months," the vision added, "you will no more of this." At the end of three months Timarchus died.

Letter V
TRANCE

The time has now arrived for expounding the phenomena of trance; an acquaintance with which is necessary to enable you to understand the source and nature of the delusions with which I have yet to deal.

You have already had glimpses of this condition. Arnod Paole was in a trance in the cemetery of Meduegna. Timarchus was in a trance in the cave of Trophonius.

Let me begin by developing certain preliminary conceptions relating to the subject.

I. The human mind is not a function of the brain, but a distinct and independent principle. It has already been shewn that the analogies of matter point to this conclusion. But there are further grounds of a merely philosophical character for its adoption. The world, as Socrates taught and Paley argued, must have been framed by a supreme intelligence; in contemplating which our reason finds no resting place short of the belief that it is eternal and selfexistent. But if the divine and infinite mind be thus essentially independent of matter, it is possible, nay analogically probable, that the human and finite mind is not less so. While many physiological phenomena favor this view, none are known which contravene it.

II. The mind through its union with the brain may be supposed to acquire a new field of experience in the suggestions of its material organs. On the other hand in this state of thraldom the mind is probably curtailed in some of the faculties of free spirit. Accordingly what we call perception is no immediate and direct apprehension of objects, but an interpretation merely, which we are instinctively led to put on our outward sensations.

III. Under ordinary circumstances the union of the mind and body is strict and absolute. Every mental faculty has its definite seat, or organ, in the nervous system; and every operation of consciousness is attended with a physical change in the organ corresponding to it. As long as these conditions hold, the relation of the mind and body is "normal."

IV. But their "abnormal" relation is conceivable; that is to say, a state, in which a part or the whole of the mental faculties may occupy unaccustomed organs; or a part even be set entirely free. The latter event seems to have been realized in the exercize of Zschokke's seer-gift; during which his apprehension took no cognisance of things around him, being lost in penetrating the inmost folds of his visitor's recollections.

V. With the exception of Zschokke's seer-gift and incidents in superstition explained through it, the phenomena which we have hitherto contemplated belong to the state of normal relation. In the production of sensorial illusions, for instance, there is no reason to suppose the normal relation of the mind and brain to be subverted.

VI. In mental delusions again there is no reason for surmising the intervention of the abnormal relation. But what are mental delusions? They are a part of insanity. And what is insanity? I will summarily state its features; for some of the instances, which remain for explanation, are referable to it; and because I delight to crush a volume into a paragraph.

The phenomena of insanity may be arranged under five heads; — the first, the insane temperament; — the three next, the fundamental forms of mental derangement; the fifth, the paroxysmal state. The features of the insane temperament are various; some of them are incompatible with the simultaneous presence of others. When a group of them is present, as a change in natural character, without insanity, insanity is threatened: no form of insanity manifests itself without the presence of some of them. The features of the insane temperament are these; the patient withdraws his sympathies from those around him, is shy, reserved, cunning, suspicious, with a troubled air as if he felt something to be wrong, and wonders if you see it; he is capricious and has flaws of temper; being talkative, he is flighty and extravagant; he is hurried in his thougths, and mode of speaking, and gestures; he is restless and anxious for change of place. Of the elementary forms of insanity, one consists in the entertainment of mental delusions; the patient imagines himself the Deity, or a prophet, or a monarch, or that he has become enormously wealthy; or that he is possessed by the devil, or is persecuted by invisible beings, or is dead, or very poor; or that he is the victim of public or private injustice. The second form is moral perversion; the patient is depressed in spirits without a cause, perhaps to the extent of meditating suicide; or he feels an unaccountable desire to take the lives of others; or he is impelled to steal, or to do gratuitous mischief; or he is a sot; or he has fits of ungovernable and dangerous rage. The third form exhibits itself in loss of connexion of ideas, loss of memory, loss of common intelligence, disregard of the common decencies of life. Each of these three elementary forms is sometimes met with alone; generally two are combined. Sensorial illusions are common in insanity; auditory, unaccompanied by visual illusions are, almost peculiar to it, and to the cognate affection of delirium from fever or inflammation of the brain. In the paroxysmal state, which is popularly termed frenzy, the patient from a more subdued condition rises into one of energetic fury or fear, wildness, agitation, attended with physical excitement; the duration of which is uncertain.

VII. In congenital idiotcy and imbecility the relation of the mind and brain is normal. Often the defective organization is apparent, through which the intelligence is repressed. In many countries a popular belief prevails that the imbecile have occasional glimpses of higher knowledge. There is no reason evident, why their minds should not be susceptible of the abnormal relation.

VIII. In sleep the mind and brain are in the normal relation. But what is sleep, psychically considered?

It is best to begin by looking into the mental constituents of waking. There is then passing before us an endless current of images and reflexions, furnished from our recollections, and suggested by our hopes and our fears, by pursuits that interest us, or by their own inter-associations. This current of thought is continually being changed or modified through impressions made upon our senses. It is further liable to be still more importantly and systematically modified by the exercize of the faculty of attention. The attention operates in a twofold manner. It enables us to detain at pleasure any subject of thought before the mind; and when not on such urgent duty, it vigilantly inspects every idea which presents itself and reports if it be palpably unsound or of questionable tendency. To speak with more precision, it is a power we have of controling our thoughts, which we drill to warn us whenever the suggested ideas conflict with our experience or our principles.

Then of sleep. We catch glimpses of its nature at the moments of falling asleep and of waking. When it is the usual time for sleep, if our attention happen to be livelily excited, it is in vain we court sleep. When we are striving to contend against the sense of overwhelming fatigue, what we feel is that we can no longer command our attention. Then we are lost, or are asleep. Then the head and body drop forwards; we have ceased to attend to the maintenance of our equilibrium. Any iteration of gentle impressions, enough to divert attention from other objects, without arousing it, promotes sleep.

Thus we recognize as the psychical basis of sleep the suspension of the attention.

Are any other mental faculties suspended in sleep? Sensation and the influence of the will over the muscular system are not. For our dreams are liable to be shaped by what we hear. The sleeper without waking will turn his head away from a bright light; will withdraw his arm if you pinch it; will utter aloud words which he dreams he is employing. The seeming insensibility in sleep, the apparent suspension of the influence of the will, are simply consequences of the suspension of attention.

I have on another occasion shewn that the organs, in which sensations are realized and volition energizes, are the segments of the cranio-spinal cord in which the sentient and voluntary nerves are rooted. I think I see now that the seat of the attention is the "medulla oblongata." Magendie observed, that when that organ is compressed, an immediate stupor supervenes. It seems to me probable that attention has its organ in that part of the medulla, which I have argued to be the dynamic centre of the nervous system.

Are the sentiments and faculties suspended during sleep?

Certainly not; if dreaming be a part of natural sleep as I hold it to be. For there are some, who dream always; others who say they seldom dream; others who disavow dreaming at all. But the simplest view of these three cases is to suppose that in sleep all persons always dream, but that all do not remember their dreams. This imputed forgetfulness is not surprizing, considering the importance of the attention to memory, and that in sleep the attention is suspended. Ordinary dreams present one remarkable feature; nothing in them appears wonderful. We meet and converse with friends long dead; the improbality of the event never crosses our minds. One sees a horse galloping by, and calls after it as one's friend M^r. so and so. We fly with agreeable facility, and explain to an admiring circle how we manage it. Every absurdity passes unchallenged. The attention is off duty. It is important to remark that there is nothing in common dreams to interfere with the purpose of sleep, which is repose. The cares and interests of our waking life never recur to us; or, if they do, are not recognized as our own. The faculties are not really energizing; their seeming exercize is sport; they are unharnessed; and are gambolling and rolling in idle relaxation. That is their refreshment.

The attention alone slumbers. Or through some slight organic change it is unlinked from the other faculties, and they are put out of gear. This is the basis of sleep. The faculties are all in their places; but the attention is off duty; itself asleep, or indolently keeping watch of time alone.

In contrast with this picture of the sleeping and waking states, of the alternation of which our mental life consists, I have now to hold up to view another conception, resembling it but different, vague, imposing, of gigantic proportions, the monstrous double of the first, — like the mocking spectre of the Hartz, which yet is but your own image cast by the level sunbeams on the morning mist.

To answer to this conception there is more than the ideal entity made up of the different forms of trance. For although trance may occur as a single sleep-like fit of moderate duration; yet it more frequently recurs; often periodically, dividing the night or day with common sleep or common waking; or it may be persistent for days and weeks; in which case, if it generally maintain one character, it is yet liable to have wakings of its own.

Then the first division of trance is into trance-sleep and trance-waking. In extreme cases it is easy to tell trance-sleep from common sleep, trance-waking from common waking; but there are varieties with less prominent features, in which it is difficult at first to say whether the patient be entranced at all.

There is upon the whole more alliance between sleep and trance, than between waking and trance. Or in a large class of cases the patient falls into trance when asleep. It is a cognate phenomenon to this that the common initiatory stage of trance is a trance-sleep.

Trance is of more frequent occurrence among the young than among the middle-aged or old people. It occurs more frequently among young women than among young men. In other words the liability to trance is in proportion to delicacy of organization and higher nervous susceptibility.

But what is trance?

The question will be best answered by exhibiting its several phases. In the meantime it may be laid down that the basis of trance is the supervention of the abnormal relation of the mind and nervous system. In almost all its forms it is easy to shew that some of the mental functions are no longer located in their pristine organs. The most ordinary change is the departure of common sensation from the organ of touch. Next, sight leaves the organs of vision. To make up for these desertions, if the patient wake in trance, either the same senses reappear elsewhere, or some unaccountable mode of general perception manifests itself.

A strict alliance exists between trance and the whole family of spasms. Most of them are exclusively developed in connexion with it; all are liable to be combined with it. One kind is catalepsy; the body motionless, statuelike, but the tone of spasm maintained low, so that you may arrange the statue in what attitude you will, and it preserves it. A second is catochus; like the preceding, but with a higher power of spasm, so that the joints are rigidly fixed; and if you overcome one for a moment with superior strength, being let go it flies back to where it was. A third; partial spasm of equal rigidity, arching the body forwards or backwards or laterally, or fixing one limb or more. The fourth, clonic spasm; for instance, the contortions and convulsive struggles of epilepsy. The fifth, an impulse to rapid and varied muscular actions, nearly equalling convulsions in violence but combined so as to travesty ordinary voluntary motion; this is the dance of St. Veitz, which took its name from an epidemic outbreak in germany in the 13th century, that was supposed to be cured by the interposition of the saint; then, persons of all classes were seized in groups in public with a fury of kicking, shuffling, dancing together, till they dropt. Now the same agency is manifested either in a violent rush and disposition to climb with inconceivable agility and precision; or alternatively, to twist the features, roll the neck, and jerk and swing the limbs even to the extent of dislocating them.

The causes of trance are mostly mental. Trance appears to be contagious. Viewed medically, it is seldom directly dangerous. It is a product of overexcitability, which time blunts. The disposition to trance (unless epilepsy, instead of being allied to, is a form of trance) is seldom manifested for more than three or four months; or in extreme cases during more than two to three years.

Of trance-sleep.

As there are three grades of ordinary sleep the heavy stupor of intense fatigue, common deep sleep, and the lightest sleep; so are there three degrees of trance-sleep. The differences of these three degrees in trance-sleep are indeed so great as to constitute them distinct conditions; but they glide into each other. The deepest trance-sleep has been already described under the title of death-trance in connexion with the subject of vampyrism. The middle grade deserves to be called trance-coma. The lightest form of trance-sleep is the common initiatory stage of trance; than which the patient may indeed advance no further. But this state is liable either to darken into the deeper forms of trance-sleep; or on the other hand to brighten into half-waking, or into whole-waking in trance; the latter mutations being the most frequent.

Two features manifest themselves in all the forms of trance-sleep. One is the apparent absence of sensation; the other the occurrence of vivid and coherent dreams. The suspension of sensation is so complete, that a limb may be amputated, even in the lightest form of trance-sleep, wihout the patient feeling it. The loudest sounds are unheard. Light has no effect upon the eyes. The dreams of trance-sleep, to which the term visions might be appropriately made over, are distinguished from those of common sleep not only by their vividness and coherence, but likewise by their bearing a direct relation to, and realizing as it were, the train of thought before uppermost in the patients mind. Thus in trance-sleep attention reappears and plays a part. Consistently with which in the lightest form of the seizure, the patient may remain either sitting, or standing, and not lose his equilibrium.

The deepest trance-sleep.

I have taken a freedom in calling the state of apparent death, in which people are liable to be buried alive, death-trance. But I am persuaded the distribution of that phenomenon under this head will prove the just one. The only feature left to be exemplified in it is the occurrence of visions. Here is an instance.

Henry Engelbrecht, as we learn in a pamphlet published by him in 1639, after an ascetic life, during which he had experienced sensorial illusions, fell into the deepest form of trance, which he thus describes; —

In the year 1623, exhausted by intense mental excitement of a religious kind and by abstinence from food, after hearing a sermon which strongly affected him, he felt as if he could combat no longer; so he gave in and took to his bed. There he lay a week without tasting any thing but the bread and wine of the sacrament. On the eighth day he thought he fell into the death-struggle. Death seemed to invade him from below upwards. His body became to his feelings rigid; his hands and feet insensible; his tongue and lips incapable of motion; gradually his sight failed him. But he still heard the laments and consultations of those around him. This gradual demise lasted from midday till eleven at night, when he heard the watchmen. Then he wholly lost sensibility to outward impressions. But an elaborate vision of immense detail began; the theme of which was, that he was first carried down to hell, and looked into the place of torment. From whence after a time, quicker than an arrow he was borne to paradise. In these abodes of suffering and happiness, he saw and heard and smelt things unspeakable. These scenes though long in apprehension were short in time; for he came enough to himself by twelve o'clock again to hear the watchmen. It took him another twelve hours to come round entirely. His hearing was first restored; then his sight; feeling and power of motion followed; as soon as he could move his limbs he rose. He felt himself stronger than before the trance.

In the middle form of trance-sleep, or trance-coma, the body lies motionless and insensible; but it is flexible. The pupils of the eyes are fixed, but not contracted as in common sleep. The circulation is regular and distinct; the breathing extremely gentle. In this state, when produced by religious excitement, dreams of a religious character occur. Trance-coma not unfrequently supervenes in hysteria, after great hysteric excitement. It may persist for days. Hysteria, it deserves to be remarked, is an irritable state of the nerves directly leading to trance, — it is, as it were, one of the vestibules to trance, figured with its own characteristic devices.

The lightest form of trance-sleep is the common initiatory stage of trance; that which forms perhaps the popular notion of trance. The patient is not necessarily recumbent. If he be sitting or standing, when taken, he may continue sitting or standing. The attention is part vigilant. The patient occasionally slightly moves in order to adjust his posture; the limbs feel to you, like those of a person awake; they make a slight resistance if you try to alter their disposition, being neither relaxed, nor yet in a state of spasm; after you have moved them they are generally replaced to where they were; they are less flexible than in common sleep. Feeling, sight, and hearing are suspended; but the patient generally appears uneasy at the near approach of any one. Later I shall have occasion further to describe the capabilities of this state. For the present I take my leave of it, with quoting a classic instance of its manifestation in the words of a writer in the Edin. Review, April, 1848.

"There is a wonderful story told of Socrates. Being in military service in the expedition to Potidea, he is reported to have stood for twenty four hours before the camp, rooted to the same spot and absorbed in deep thought, his arms folded, and his eyes fixed upon one object, as if his soul were absent from his body."

Letter VI
SOMNAMBULISM

A curious fate somnambulism has had. While other forms of trance have been either rejected as fictions, or converted to the use of superstition, somnambulism with all its wonders, being at once undeniable and familiar, has been simply taken for granted. While her sisters have been exalted into mystical phenomena, and play parts in history, somnambulism has had no temple raised to her, has had no fear-worship, at the highest has been promoted to figure in an opera. Of a quiet and homely nature she has moved about the house, not like a visiting demon, but as a maid of all work. To the public the phenomenon has presented no more interest than a soap-bubble or the fall of an apple.

Somnambulism, as the term is used in England, exactly comprehends all the phenomena of half-waking trance. The seizure mostly comes on during common sleep. But it may supervene in the day-time; in which case the patient first falls into the lightest form of trance-sleep. After a little, still lost to things around him, he manifests three impulses; one, to speak, but coherently and to a purpose; a second, to dress, rise, and leave his room with an evident intention of going somewhither; a third, to practise some habitual mechanical employment. In each case he appears to be pursuing the thread of a dream. If he speaks, it is a connected discourse to some end. If he goes out to walk, it is to a spot he contemplates visiting; his general turn is to climb ascents, hills or the roofs of houses; in the latter case he sometimes examines if the tiles are secure before he steps on them. If he pursues a customary occupation, whether it be cleaning harness or writing music, he finishes his work before he leaves it. He is acting a dream, which is connected and sustained. The attention is keenly awake in this dream, and favors its accomplishment to the utmost. In the mean time the somnambulist appears to be insensible to ordinary impressions, and to take no cognizance of what is going on around him; a light may be held so close to his eyes as to singe his eyebrows without his noticing it; he seems neither to hear nor to taste; the eyelids are generally closed; otherwise the eyes are fixed and vacant. Nevertheless he possesses some means of recognizing the objects, which are implicated in his dream; he perceives their place, and walks among them with perfect precision. Let me narrate some instances. The first, one of day-somnambulism, exemplifies at the same time the transitions to whole-waking, which manifest themselves occasionally in the talking form of the trance. The case is from the acta Vratis v. ann. 1722.

A girl seventeen years of age was used to fall into a kind of sleep in the afternoon, in which it was supposed from her expression of countenance and her gestures, that she was engaged in dreams that interested her. (She was then in light trance-sleep, initiatory trance.) After some days she began to speak when in this state Then if those present addressed remarks to her she replied very sensibly; but then fell back into her dream-discourse; which turned principally upon religious and moral topics, and was directed to warn her friends how a female should live, christianly, well-governed, and so as to incur no reproach. When she sang, which often happened, she heard herself accompanied by an imaginary violin or piano, and would take up and continue the accompaniment upon an instrument herself. She sewed, did knitting, and the like. She imagined on one occasion that she wrote a letter upon a napkin, which she folded for the post. Upon waking she had not the slightest recollection of any thing that had passed. After a few months she recovered.

The following case is from the Hamburg Zeitschrift für die gesammte Medicin. 1848.

A lad of eleven years of age, at school at Tarbes, was surprized several mornings running at finding himself dressed in bed, tho' he had undrest himself overnight. Then on the 3ᵈ of May he was seen by a neighbour, soon after three in the morning, to go out dressed with his cloak and hat on. She called to him, but he did not answer; and she concluded that he was going to Bagnères with his father. In fact that was the road he took; and he was afterwards seen by several persons near Bagnères trudging after a carriage. It rained hard; and they were surprized to see so young a lad travelling at so early an hour; but they thought he probably belonged to the people in the carriage. He reached Bagnères at half past five, having done the distance of five post leagues in two hours and a quarter. He went to the hotel of M. Lafargue, which he had on a former occasion visited with his father, and entered the eatingroom. The people of the hotel addressed him. He told them that he had come with his father in a postchaise, and that they would find his father in the yard busied with the carriage. M. Lafargue went out to look for him. In the mean time the people of the house observed that the boy's remarks were incoherent; so they took off his cloak and cap; when they found that his eyelids were closed and that he was fast asleep. They led him towards the stove, took off his wet things and his boots without awakening him; but before they had completely undressed him to put him to bed, he woke.

The impressions of his dream did not desert him. He complained of having had a bad night; and asked for his father. They told him his father had been obliged to set off again immediately. They put him to bed and he slept. They sent intelligence to his father, who came to Bagnères. The boy believed and believes still, that he came to Bagnères with his father in a chaise that was driven very slowly. Being asked what he had seen on the road he described having passed a number of monks and priests in procession. He said there was one good-looking young man, who did not leave him, but was always saying. "Good day, Joseph; Adieu, Joseph." He said that what had most annoyed him was the burning heat of the sun, which was so intense that he had been obliged to wrap himself up in his cloak; that he could not bear its bright light. —

The following case of somnabulism allied with St. Veitz's dance is given by Lord Monboddo.

The patient, about sixteen years of age, used to be commonly taken in the morning a few hours after rising. The approach of the seizure was announced by a sense of weight in the head and drowziness, which quickly terminated in sleep (trance-sleep), in which her eyes were fast shut. She described a feeling beginning in the feet, creeping like a gradual chill higher and higher, till it reached the heart, when consciousness left her. Being in this state she sprang from her seat about the room, over tables and chairs with astonishing agility. Then if she succeeded in getting out of the house, she ran at a pace with which her elder brother could hardly keep up to a particular spot in the neighbourhood, taking the directest but the roughest path. If she could not manage otherwise, she got over the garden-wall, with astonishing rapidity and precision of movement. Her eyelids were all the time fast closed. The impulse to visit this spot she was often conscious of during the approach of the paroxysm, and afterwards she sometimes thought that she had dreamed of going thither. Towards the termination of her indisposition, she dreamed that the water of a neighbouring spring would do her good, and she drank much of it. One time they tried to cheat her by giving her water from another spring; but she immediately detected the difference. Near the end, she foretold that she would have three paroxysms more, and then be well; — and so it proved.

The next case is from a communication by M. Pigatti, published in the July number of the journal encyclopédique of the year 1662. The subject was a servant of the name of Negretti, in the household of the Marquis Sale.

In the evening Negretti would seat himself in a chair in the ante-room, when he commonly fell asleep, and would sleep quietly for a quarter of an hour. He then righted himself in his chair so as to sit up. Then he sat sometime without motion looking as if he saw something. Then he rose and walked about the room. On one occasion he drew out his snuff-box and would have taken a pinch but there was little in it; whereupon he walked up to an empty chair, and addressing by name a cavalier, whom he supposed to be sitting in it, asked him for a pinch. One of those, who were watching the scene, here held towards him an open box, from which he took snuff. Afterwards he fell into the posture of a person who listens; he seemed to think that he heard an order, and thereupon hastened with a wax-candle in his hand to a spot where a light usually stood. As soon as he imagined that he had lit the candle, he walked with it in the proper manner, through the salle, down the steps turning and waiting from time to time, as if he were lighting some one down. Arrived at the door he placed himself sideways, in order to let the imaginary persons pass, and he bowed as he let them out. He then extinguished the light, returned up the stairs, and sat himself down again in his place, to play the same farce once or twice over again the same evening. When in this condition he would lay the table-cloth, place the chairs, which he sometimes brought from a distant room, opening and shutting the doors as he went with exactness; would take decanters from the buffet, fill them with water at the spring, put them down on a waiter and so on. All the objects that were concerned in these operations he distinguished when they were before him with the same precision and certainty as if he had been in the full use of his senses. Otherwise he seemed to observe nothing; so on one occasion in passing a table, he threw down a waiter with two decanters upon it, which fell and broke without attracting his attention. The dominant idea had entire possession of him. He would prepare a salad with correctness, and sit down and eat it. If they changed it, the trick escaped his notice. In this manner he would go on eating cabbage or even pieces of cake without observing the difference. The taste he enjoyed was imaginary, the sense was shut. On another occasion when he asked for wine, they gave him water which he drank for wine, and remarked that his stomach felt the better for it. On a fellow-servant touching his legs with a stick, the idea arose in his mind, that it was a dog; and he scolded to drive it away. But the servant continuing his game, Negretti took a whip to beat the dog. The servant drew back, when Negretti began whistling and coaxing to get the dog near him; so they threw a muff against his legs, which he belabored soundly.

M. Pigatti watched these proceedings with great attention, and convinced himself by many experiments that Negretti did not use his ordinary senses. He did not hear the loudest sound when it lay out of the circle of his dream ideas. If a light was held close to his eyes near enough to singe his eyebrows, he did not appear to be aware of it. He seemed to feel nothing when they inserted a feather into his nostrils.

Perhaps the most interesting case of somnabulism on record is that of a young ecclesiastic, the narrative of which from the immediate communication of the Archbishop of Bordeaux is given under the head of somnambulism in the french encyclopedia.

This young ecclesiastic, when the archbishop was at the same seminary, used to rise every night, and write out either sermons or pieces of music. To study his condition, the archbishop betook himself several nights consecutively to the chamber of the young man, where he made the following observations.

The young man used to rise, take paper, and begin to write. Before writing music he would take a stick and rule the lines with it. He wrote the notes together with the words corresponding to them with perfect correctness, or, when he had written the words too wide, he altered them. The notes that were to be black, he filled in after he had written the whole. After completing a sermon, he would read it aloud from beginning to end. If any passage displeased him, he erased it, and wrote the amended passage correctly over the other; on one occasion he had substituted the word "adorable" for "divin;" but he did not omit to alter the preceding "ce" into "cet," by adding the letter "t" with exact precision to the word first written. To ascertain whether he used his eyes, the archbishop interposed a sheet of pasteboard between the writing and his face. The somnabulist took not the least notice, but went on writing as before. The limitation of his perceptions to what he was thinking about was very curious. A bit of aniseed cake, that he had sought for, he eat approvingly; but when on another occasion, a piece of the same cake was put into his mouth; he spat it out without observation. The following instance of the dependence of his perceptions upon his preconceived ideas is truly wonderful. It is to be observed that he always knew when his pen had ink in it. Likewise, if they adroitly changed his papers when he was writing he knew it, if the sheet substituted was of a different size from the former, and he appeared embarrassed in that case. But if the fresh sheet of paper, which was substituted for that written on, was exactly of the same size with it, he appeared not to be aware of the change. And he would continue to read off his composition from the blank sheet of paper, as fluently as when the manuscript lay before him; nay more, he would continue his corrections, and introduce ar amended passage writing it upon exactly the place in the blank sheet corresponding with that, which it would have occupied in the written page. — Such are the feats of somnabulists.

At first sight the phenomena thus exemplified appear strange and unintelligible enough. But upon a careful consideration of them much of the marvellous disappears. The most curious features seem in the end to be really the least deserving of wonder. The simplest of the phenomena are alone the inexplicable ones.

I have however advanced this group of cases as

instances of trance, in which therefore I pretend that an abnormal relation exists between the mind and body, in which the organs of sensation are partially or entirely deserted by their functions, and in which new perceptive powers manifest themselves. Then an opponent might argue; —

"I know nothing about your trance. What I see is first a person asleep, then the same person half or partially awake, occupied with a dream or vivid conception of an action; which, being partially awake, and therefore having partially resumed his power of attention, he is capable of realizing. He appears to be insensible; but this may be deceptive; for he is still asleep and therefore notices not things around him; and his attention is partly still suspended as in sleep, partly more useless still for general purposes through intent preoccupation."

"He goes about the house in his rapt state and finds his way perfectly; but the house is familiar to him; every thing in it is distinctly before his conception; he has too the advantage of perfect confidence; and besides, being partially awake, he partially, vaguely perhaps, uses customary sensations in reference to the objects, which his dream contemplates his meeting."

"The ecclesiastic indeed seems at first to see through a sheet of pasteboard. But the concluding interesting fact in his case shews that he really used his perception only to identify the size and place of the sheet of paper. His writing upon it was the mechanical transcript of an act of mental penmanship. The corrections fell into the right places upon the paper owing to the fidelity with which he retained the mental picture. The clearness and vividness of the picture again is not so very surprising, when it is considered that the attention was wholly and exclusively concentrated on that one operation."

The observations of my imaginary opponent might

sufficiently account for the more striking phenomena in the preceding cases, and are doubtless near the truth as regards the principal parts of the young ecclesiastic's performance. Still there remains the commoner instance of the lad going about with precision with his eyes shut. I see no mode of accounting for that on common principles.

And besides, it may be presumed that if more decisive experiments as to their sensibility had been made upon all these subjects, they would have been found really without sight and feeling. For in general character persons in somnambulism exactly resemble other entranced persons, who certainly feel nothing; for they have borne the most painful surgical operations without the smallest indication of suffering. So I have little doubt that the insensibility, which the observers imputed to the somnambulists, really existed, altho' they may have failed to establish the fact by positive evidence.

The question as to the development of a new power of perception, such as I conjecture the lad used in his walk from Tarbes to Barèges, will be found to be resolved, or at any rate to be attended with no theoretical difficulties, when the performances of full-waking in trance, which I propose to describe in the next letter, shall have laid before the reader.

Letter VII
CATALEPSY

Under this head are contained the most marvellous phenomena which ever came as a group of facts in natural philosophy before the world. And they are reaching that stage towards general reception, when their effect is most vivid and striking. Five and twenty years ago no one in England dreamed of believing them, altho' the same positive evidence of their genuineness then existed as now. Five and twenty years hence the same facts will be matters of familiar knowledge. It is just at the present moment (or am I anticipating the march of opinion by half a century?) that their difference, and distinctness, and abhorrence even, from our previous conceptions are most intensely felt; and that the powers which they promise eventually to place within human control excite our irrepressible wonder.

I shall narrate the facts, which loom so large in the dawning light, very simply and briefly. They are manifested in catalepsy.

An uninformed person being in the room with a cataleptic patient, would at first suppose her, putting aside the spasmodic affection of the body, to be simply awake in the ordinary way. By and bye her new powers might or might not catch his observation. But a third point would certainly escape his notice. I refer to her mental state of waking trance, which gives as it were the local coloring to the whole performance.

To elucidate this element, I may avail myself of a sketch ready prepared by nature, tinted with the local colour alone, the case of simple trance-waking, unattended by fits or by any marvellous powers as far as it has been yet observed, which is known to physicians under the name of double consciousness.

A single fit of the disorder presents the following features. The young person (for the patient is most frequently a girl) seems to lose herself for a moment or longer, then she recovers, and seems to be herself again. The intervening short period, longer at first, and by use rendered briefer and briefer, is a period of common initiatory trance. When, having lost, the patient thus finds herself again, there is nothing in her behaviour, which would lead a stranger to suppose her other than naturally awake. But her friends observe that she now does every thing with more spirit and better than before, sings better, plays better, has more readiness, moves even more gracefully, than in her usual state. She manifests an innocent boldness and disregard of little conventionalisms, which impart a peculiar charm to her behaviour. Her mode of speaking is perhaps something altered; a supernumerary consonant making its undue appearance, but upon a regular law, in certain syllables. But the most striking thing is that she has totally forgotten all that has passed during the morning. Inquire what her last recollections are, they leave off with the termination of her last fit of this kind; the intervening period is for the present lost to her. — She was in her natural state of waking, when I introduced her to your notice; she lost herself for a few seconds; found herself again, but found herself not in her natural train of recollections, but in those of the last fit.

These fits occur sometimes at irregular intervals, sometimes periodically and daily. In her ordinary waking state, she has her chain of waking recollections. In her trance-waking state, she has her chain of trance-waking recollections. The two are kept strictly apart. Hence the ill-chosen term, double-consciousness. So at the occurrence of her first fit her mental existence may be said to have bifurcated into two separate routes, in either of which her being is alternately passed. It is curious to study at the commencement of such a case with how much knowledge derived from her past life the patient embarks on her trance-existence. The number of previously realized ideas retained by different patients at the first fit is very various. It has happened that the memory of facts and persons has been so defective, that the patient has had to learn even to know and to love her parents. To most of her acquaintances she is observed to give new names, which she uses to them in the trance-state alone. But her habits remain; her usual propriety of conduct; the mind is singularly pure in trance. And she very quickly picks up former ideas, and restores former intimacies but on a supposed new footing. To complete this curious history, if the fits of trance recur frequently, and through some accidental circumstance are more and more prolonged in duration, so that most of her waking existence is passed in trance, it will follow that the trance-development of her intellect and character may get ahead of their development in her natural waking. Being told this she may become anxious to continue always in her entranced state, and to drop the other; and I knew a case, in which circumstances favoured this final arrangement; and the patient at last retained her trance-recollections alone, from long continuances in that state having made it as it were her natural one. Her only fear was, for she had gradually learned her own mental history, as she expressed it to me, that some day she should of a sudden find herself a child again, thrown back to the point at which she ceased her first order of recollections. This is indeed a very extreme and monstrous case. Ordinarily the recurrence of fits of simple trance-waking does not extend over a longer period than three or four months or half a year; after which they never reappear; and her trance-acquirements and feelings are lost to the patient's recollection for good. I will cite a case, as it was communicated to me by Dr. G. Barlow exemplifying some of the points of the preceding statement.

"This young lady has two states of existence. During the time that the fit is on her, which varies from a few hours to three days, she is occasionally merry and in spirits; occasionally she appears in pain and rolls about in uneasiness; but in general she seems so much herself, that a stranger entering the room would not remark any thing extraordinary; she amuses herself with reading or working, sometimes plays on the piano and better than at other times, knows every body, and converses rationally, and makes very accurate observations on what she has seen and read. The fit leaves her suddenly, and she then forgets every thing that has passed during it, and imagines that she has been asleep, and sometimes that she has dreamed of any circumstance that has made a vivid impression upon her. During one of these fits she was reading Miss Edgeworth's tales, and had in the morning been reading a part of one of them to her mother, when she went for a few minutes to the window, and suddenly exclaimed, Mamma, I am quite well, my headach is gone.' Returning to the table, she took up the open volume, which she had been reading five minutes before, and said, 'What book is this?' she turned over the leaves, looked at the frontispiece, and replaced it on the table. Seven or eight hours afterwards, when the fit returned, she asked for the book, went on at the very paragraph where she had left off, and remembered every circumstance of the narrative. And so it always is; as she reads one set of books during one state, and another during the other. She seems to be conscious of her state; for she said one day, 'Mamma, this is a novel, but I may safely read it; it will not hurt my morals, for, when I am well, I shall not remember a word of it.'"

To form a just idea of a case of catalepsy, the reader has to imagine such a case as I have just instanced with the physical feature added that the patient when entranced is motionless and fixed as a statue; the spasmodic state however not confining itself closely to one type, but running into catochus, or into partial rigid spasm, (see letter V) capriciously.

The psychical phenomena exhibited by her when thus entranced are the following.

1. The organs of sensation are deserted by their natural sensibility. The patient neither feels with the skin, nor sees with the eyes, nor hears with the ears, nor tastes with the mouth.

2. All these senses, however, are not lost. Sight and hearing, if not smell and taste, reappear in some other part; at the pit of the stomach for instance, or the tips of the fingers,

3. The patient manifests new perceptive powers. She discerns objects all around her and through any obstructions, partitions, walls or houses, and at an indefinite distance. She sees her own inside as it were illuminated, and can tell what is wrong in the health of others. She reads the thoughts of others whether present or at indefinite distances. The ordinary obstacles of space and matter vanish to her. So likewise that of time; she foresees future events.

Such and more are the capabilities of cataleptic patients, most of whom exhibit them all; — but there is some caprice in their manifestation.

I first resigned myself to the belief that such statements as the above might be true, upon being shewn by the late Mr. Bulteel letters from an eminent provincial physician in the year 1838, describing phenomena of this description in a patient the latter was attending. In the spring of 1839 Mr. Bulteel told me that he had himself in the interim often seen the patient, who had allowed him to test in any way he pleased the reality of the faculties she possessed when entranced. As usual in the hours which she passed daily in her natural state she had no recollection of her extraordinary trance performances. The following are some of the facts, which Mr. Bulteel told me he had himself verified.

When entranced the patient's expression of countenance was slightly altered, and there was some peculiarity in her mode of speaking. To each of her friends she had given a new name, which she used only when in the state of trance. She could read with her skin. If she pressed the palm of her hand against the whole surface of a printed page deliberately, as it were to take off an impression, she became acquainted verbally with its contents, even to the extent of criticising the type or the handwriting. One day after a remark made to put her off her guard, a line of a folded note was pressed against the back of her neck; she had read it. She called this sense feeling; contact was necessary for its manifestation. But she had a general perceptive power besides. She used to tell that persons, whom she knew, were coming to the house, when they were yet at some distance. Persons sitting in the room with her playing chess, to whom her back was turned, if they made intentionally false moves, she would smile and ask them what they possibly could do that for.

The three next cases, which I shall describe are from a memoir on catalepsy (1787) by Dr. Petetin, an eminent civil and military physician at Lyons.

M. Petetin attended a young married lady in a sort of fit. She lay seemingly unconscious; when he raised her arm, it remained in the air where he placed it. Being put to bed, she commenced singing. To stop her, the doctor placed her limbs each in a different position. This embarrassed her considerably, but she went on singing. She seemed perfectly insensible. Pinching the skin, shouting in her ear, nothing aroused her attention. Then it happened that, in arranging her, the doctor's foot slipped; and, as he recovered himself, half leaning over her, he said, "how provoking we can't make her leave off singing!" "Ah, doctor," she cried, "don't be angry! I won't sing any more," and she stopped. But shortly she began again; and in vain did the doctor implore her, by the loudest entreaties, addressed to her ear, to keep her promise and desist. It then occurred to him to place himself in the same position as when she heard him before. He raised the bed-clothes, bent his head towards her stomach, and said, in a loud voice, "Do you, then, mean to sing for ever?" "Oh, what pain you have given me!" she exclaimed — "I implore you speak lower;" at the same time she passed her hand over the pit of her stomach. "In what way, then, do you hear?" said Dr. Petetin. "Like any one else," was the answer. "But I am speaking to your stomach." "Is it possible!" she said. He then tried again whether she could hear with her ears, speaking even through a tube to aggravate his voice; — she heard nothing. On his asking her, at the pit of her stomach, if she had not heard him, — "No," said she, "I am indeed unfortunate."

A cognate phenomenon to the above is *the conversion of the patient's new sense of vision in a direction inwards*. He looks into himself, and sees his own inside as it were illuminated or transfigured. That is to say, his visual power is turned inwards; and he sees his organs by the Od-light they give out.

A few days after the scene just described, Dr. Petetin's patient had another attack of catalepsy. She still heard at the pit of her stomach, but the manner of hearing was modified. In the mean time her countenance expressed astonishment. Dr. Petetin inquired the cause. "It is not difficult," she answered, "to explain to you why I look astonished. I am singing, doctor, to divert my attention from a sight which appals me. I see my inside, and the strange forms of the organs, surrounded with a network of light. My countenance must express what I feel, — astonishment and fear. A physician who should have my complaint for a quarter of an hour would think himself fortunate, as nature would reveal all her secrets to him. If he was devoted to his profession, he would not, as I do, desire to be quickly well." "Do you see your heart?" asked Dr. Petetin. "Yes, there it is; it beats at twice; the two sides in agreement; when the upper part contracts, the lower part swells, and immediately after that contracts. The blood rushes out all luminous, and issues by two great vessels which are but a little apart."

One morning (to quote from the latter part of this case), the access of the fit took place, according to custom, at eight o'clock. Petetin arrived later than usual; he announced himself by speaking to the fingers of the patient (by which he was heard). "You are a very lazy person this morning, doctor," said she. "It is true, madam; but if you knew the reason, you would not reproach me." "Ah," said she, "I perceive, you have had a headach for the last four hours; it will not leave you till six in the evening. You are right to take nothing; no human means can prevent its running its course." "Can you tell me on which side is the pain?" said Petetin. "On the right side; it occupies the temple, the eye, the teeth: I warn you that it will invade the left eye, and that you will suffer considerably between three and four o'clock; at six you will be free from pain." The prediction came out literally true. "If you wish me to believe you, you must tell me what I hold in my hand?" "I see through your hand an antique medal."

Petetin inquired of his patient at what hour her own fit would cease: "at eleven." "And the evening accession, when will it come on?" "At seven o'clock." "In that case it will be later than usual." "It is true;

the periods of its recurrence are going to change to so and so." During this conversation, the patient's countenance expressed annoyance. She then said to M. Petetin, "My uncle has just entered; he is conversing with my husband, behind the screen; his visit will fatigue me, beg him to go away." The uncle, leaving, took with him by mistake her husband's cloak, which she perceived, and sent her sister-inlaw to reclaim it.

In the evening, there were assembled, in the lady's apartment, a good number of her relations and friends. Petetin had, intentionally, placed a letter within his waistcoat, on his heart. He begged permission, on arriving, to wear his cloak. Scarcely had the lady, the access having come on, fallen into trance, when she said, — 'And how long, doctor, has it come into fashion to wear letters next the heart?" Petetin pretended to deny the fact; she insisted on her correctness; and, raising her hands, designated the size, and indicated exactly the place of the letter. Petetin drew forth the letter, and held it, closed, to the fingers of the patient. "If I were not a discreet person," she said, "I should tell the contents; but to show you that I know them, they form exactly two lines and a half of writing;" which, on opening the letter, was shown to be the fact.

A friend of the family, who was present, took out his purse and put it in Dr. Petetin's bosom, and folded his cloak over his chest. As soon as Petetin approached his patient, she told him that he had the purse, and named its exact contents. She then gave an inventory of the contents of the pockets of all present; adding some pointed remark when the opportunity offered. She said to her sister-in-law that the most interesting thing in *her* possession was a letter; — much to her surprise, for she had received the letter the same evening, and had mentioned it to no one.

The patient, in the mean time, lost strength daily, and could take no food. The means employed failed of giving her relief, and it never occurred to M. Petetin to inquire of her how he should treat her. At length, with some vague idea that she suffered from too great electric tension of the brain, he tried, fantastically enough, the effect of making deep inspirations, standing close in front of the patient. No effect followed from this absurd proceeding. Then he placed one hand on the forehead, the other on the pit of the stomach of the patient, and continued his inspirations. The patient now opened her eyes; her features lost their fixed look; she rallied rapidly from the fit, which lasted but a few minutes instead of the usual period of two hours more. In eight days, under a pursuance of this treatment, she entirely recovered from her fits, and with them ceased her extraordinary powers. But, during these eight days, her powers manifested a still greater extension; she foretold what was going to happen to her; she discussed, with astonishing subtlety, questions of mental philosophy and physiology; she caught what those around her meant to say, before they expressed their wishes, and either did what they desired, or begged that they would not ask her to do what was beyond her strength.

A young lady, after much alarm during a revolutionary riot, fell into catalepsy. In her fits she appeared to hear with the pit of the stomach; and most of the phenomena described in the preceding case were again manifested. She improved in health under the care of Dr. Petetin up to the 29th of May 1790, the memorable day when the inhabitants of Lyons expelled the wretches who were making sport of their fortunes, their liberties, and their lives. At the report of the first cannon fired, Mlle — fell into violent convulsions followed by catalepsy and tetanus. When in this state, she discerned Petetin distinguishing himself under the fire of a battery; and she blamed him the following day for having so rashly exposed his life. In the progress of the complaint, during the attacks of catalepsy, the recurrences of which she exactly foresaw, she likewise predicted the bloody day of the 29th of September, the surrender of the city on the 7th of October, the entrance of the republican troops on the 8th, and the cruel proscriptions issued by the committee of public safety.

The third case given by Petetin is that of Madame de Saint-Paul who was attacked with catalepsy a few days after her marriage in consequence of seeing her father fall down in a fit of apoplexy at table. The general features of her lucidity are the same as in the former cases. I shall therefore, content myself with quoting some observations made by Dr. Prost, author of "la medecine eclairée par l'observation et l'anatomie pathologique," on the authority of Dr. Foissac, to whom he communicated them. Dr. Prost had studied this case assiduously during nine months. "Her intellectual faculties," observed Dr. Prost, "acquired a great activity, and the richness of her fancy made itself remarked in the picturesque images which she threw into her descriptions. As she was telling her friends of an approaching attack of catalepsy, suddenly she exclaimed, 'I no longer see or hear objects in the same manner, every thing is transparent round me and my observation extends to incalculable distances.' She designated without an error the people who were on the public promenade, whether near the house, or still a quarter of an hour's walk distant. She read the thoughts of every one who came near her; she marked those who were false and vicious; and repelled the approach of stupid people, who bored her with their questions and aggravated her malady. 'Just as much as their pates excite my pity,' said she, 'do the heads of men of information and intelligence, all whose thoughts I look into, fill me with delight.'

The following facts I cite corroboratively from one of several cases of hysteria communicated by Dr. Delpit, inspecting physician of the waters at Barèges. Bibliotheque medicale. T. LVI. p. 308.

Mlle V., aged thirteen, after seeing the curé administer extreme unction fainted away. There followed extreme disgust towards food. During eighteen days she neither eat nor drank; there was no secretion; her breathing remained tranquil and regular; the patient preserved her embonpoint and complexion. During this complete suspension of the functions of digestion, the organs of sensation would be alternately paralysed. One day the patient became blind; on the next she could see but could not hear; another day she lost her speech. The mutations were noticed generally in the night upon her waking out of sleep. "Nevertheless," says M. Delpit, "her intellect preserved all its vivacity and force; and during the palsy of the organs of sensation nature supplied the loss in another way; when with her eyes Mlle Caroline could not distinguish light, she yet read, and read distinctly, by carrying her fingers over the letters. I have made her thus read in the day-time, and in the profoundest darkness, either printed pages out of the first book that came to hand, or written passages that I had previously prepared."

Sensorial illusions occasionally occur in catalepsy; but not frequently; they are commoner in the inferior grades of trance. The daimon of Socrates was no doubt an hallucination of this kind.

The trance-daimon, or sensorial illusion mixing itself with trance, is exemplified in the following case of catalepsy which occurred in the person of the adopted daughter of the Baron de Strombeck.

Besides the ordinary features, on which I will not again dwell, at one time it was her custom to apply to an imaginary being for directions as to the treatment of her own case. Subsequently she one day observed, "it is not a phantom; I was in error in thinking it so; it is a voice, which speaks within me, and which I think without me. This apparition comes because my sleep is less perfect. In that case I seem to see a white cloud rise out of the earth, from which a voice issues, the echo of which reverberates within me."

This patient had quintuple consciousness, or four morbid states, each of which kept its own recollections to itself.

A final case I will quote, the authority or which is the Baron de Fortis. It was treated by Dr. Despine of Aix-les-Bains.

The patient had had epilepsy, for the cure of which she went to Aix; there she had all sorts of fits; and day-somnabulism, during which she waited at table, with her eyes shut, perfectly. She likewise saw alternately with her fingers, the palm of her hand, and her elbow; and would write with precision with her right hand, superintending the process with her left elbow. These details are particularly gratifying to myself, for in the little I have seen, I yet have seen a patient walk about with her eyes shut and well blinded besides, holding the knuckles of one hand before her as a seeing lantern. However the special interest of this case is that the patient was differently affected by different kinds of matter; glass appeared to burn her; porcelaine was pleasantly warm; earthen-ware felt cold.

What comment can I make on the preceding wondrous details? Those, to whom they are new, must have time to become familiar with them; in order, reversing the process by which the eye gets to see in the dark, to learn to distinguish objects in this flood of excessive light. Those who are already acquainted with them, will I think agree with me, that the principle which I have assumed, — the possibility of an abnormal relation of the mind and body allowing the former, either to shift the place of its manifestations in the nervous system, or partially to energize as free spirit, — is the only one, which at present offers any solution of the new powers displayed in catalepsy. One regrets that more was not made of the opportunities of observation, which Petetin enjoyed. But there are means, which I shall by and by have occasion to specify, through which in the practice of medicine and in the proper treatment of various disorders, like instances may be artificially multiplied and modified so as to meet the exigencies of inductive science. In the mean time let me append one or two corollaries to the preceding demonstration.

I. It is evident that the performances of catalepsy reduce the oracles of antiquity to natural phenomena. Let us examine the tradition of that of Delphi.

Diodorus relates that goats feeding near an opening in the ground were observed to jump about in a singular manner, and that a goatherd approaching to examine the spot was taken with a fit and prophecied. Then the priests took possession of the spot and built a temple. Plutarch tells us that the priestess was an uneducated peasant-girl, of good character and conduct. Placed upon the tripod and affected by the exhalation, she struggled and became convulsed and foamed at the mouth; and in that state she delivered the oracular answer. The convulsions were sometimes so violent that the Pythia died. Plutarch adds that the answers were never in error; and that their established truth filled the temple with offerings from the whole of Greece and from barbarian nations. — Without supposing it to have been infallible we must I think infer that the oracle was too often right to have been wholly a trick. The state of the Pythia was probably trance with convulsions, the same with that in which cataleptic patients have foreseen future events. The priestess was of blameless life; which suits the production of trance; the fine susceptibility of which is spoilt by irregular living. Finally from what we know of the effects of the few gases and vapors, of which the inhalation has been tried, it is any thing but improbable that one or other gazeous compound should directly induce trance in predisposed subjects.

III. The performances of Zschokke are poor by the side of those of a cataleptic. But he was not absolutely entranced. Nevertheless an approach to that state manifested itself in his losing himself when inspecting his visitor's brains. So again those who had the gift of second-sight are represented to have been subject to fits of abstraction, in which they stood rapt. The praeternatural gifts of Socrates were probably those of a Highland seer. In which character he is reported to have foretold the death of an officer, if he pursued a route he contemplated: the officer would not change his plans, and was met by the enemy and slain accordingly. In all these cases the mind seems to have gone out to seek its knowledge. Two of Mr. Williamson's lucid patients, of whom more afterwards, told him that their minds went out at the backs of their heads in starting on these occasions. They pointed to the lower and back part of the head, opposite to the Medulla oblongata. In prophetic and in true retrospective dreams one may imagine the phenomena taking the same course; most likely the dreamers have slipt in their sleep into a brief lucid somnambulism. In the cases of ghosts and of dreams coincident with the period of the death of an absent person, it seems simpler to suppose the visit to have come from the other side. So the Vampyr-ghost was probably a visit made by the free part of the mind of the patient who lay buried in death-trance. The visit was fatal to the party visited, because trance is contagious.

III. The instinct of animals appears less incomprehensible when viewed in juxta-position with some of the feats of lucid cataleptics. The term instinct is a very vague one. It is commonly used to denote the intelligence of animals as opposed to human reason. Instinct is therefore a compound phenomenon; and I must begin by resolving it into its elements; they are three in number; —

1. Observation and reasoning of the same kind with that of man, but incomparably more limited in their scope and reach. They are exercized only in immediate self-preservation and in the direct supply of the creatures bodily wants or simple impulses. A dog will whine to get admission into the house; will open the latch of a gate; one rook will sit sentry for the rest; a plover will fly low and short distances, as if hurt, to wile a dog away from her nest. But in this vein of intelligence animals make no further advance. Reflexion with the higher faculties and sentiments, which minister to it, and with it constitute reason, is denied them. So they originate no objects of pursuit in the way that man does, and have no source of self-improvement. But in lack of human reflection some animals receive the help of —

2. special conceptions, which are developed in their minds at fitting seasons. Of this nature is the notion of nest-building in birds. It may be observed of these conceptions that they appear to us arbitrary, tho' perfectly suited to the being of each species; the material and shape of the nest for instance might be varied without its object being the less perfectly attained, at least as far as we can see.

The conception spontaneously developed in the mind of the bird is then carried out intelligently through the same quick and just observation in a little way, which ministers to its appetites, as I explained in a preceding paragraph. The special conception is sometimes characterized by the utmost perfectness of mechanical design. Here, however, is nothing to surprize us. The supreme wisdom which pre-ordained the development of an idea in an insect's mind might as easily as not have given it absolute perfectness. But —

3. some animals have the power of modifying the special conception, when circumstances arise which prevent its being carried out in the usual way; and of realizing it in a great many different ways on as many different occasions. And their work on each of these occasions is as perfect as in their carrying out the ordinary form of the conception. I beg leave to call the principle, by which they see thus how to shape their course so perfectly under new circumstances intuition. To instance it. There is a beetle called the rhynchites betula. Its habit is towards the end of May to cut the leaves of the betula alba or betula pubescens, into slips which it rolls up into funnel-shaped chambers which form singularly convenient cradles for its eggs. This is done after one pattern, — and one may suppose it the mechanichal realization of an inborn idea — as long as the leaf is perfect in shape. But if the leaf is imperfect, intuition steps upon the scene, to aid the insect to cut its coat after its cloth. The sections made are then seen to vary with the varying shape of the leaf. Many different sections made by the insect were accurately drawn by a german naturalist, Dr. Debey. He submitted them for examination to Professor Heis of Aix-la-Chapelle. Upon carefully studying them Dr. Heis found these cuttings of the leaves, in suitableness to the end proposed

even to the minutest technical detail, to be in accordance with calculations compassable only through the higher mathematics, which till modern times were unknown to human intelligence. Such is the marvellous power of "intuition," displayed by certain insects. I know not how to define it but as a power of immediate reference to absolute truth evinced by the insect in carrying out its little plans. It is evident that the insect uses the same power in realizing its ordinary special conception, when the result displays equal perfectness. And the question even crosses ones mind, are the seemingly arbitrary plans really arbitrary, may they not equally represent an highest type of design? But be that as it may, the intuition of insects as we now apprehend it, no longer stands an isolated phenomenon. The lucid cataleptic can not less directly communicate with the source of truth, as she proves by foreseeing future events.

IV. The speculations of Berkeley and Boscovich on the non-existence of matter; and of Kant and others on the arbitrariness of all our notions; are interested in, for they appear to be refuted by, the intuitions of cataleptics. The cataleptic apprehends or perceives directly the objects around her; — but they are the same as when realized through her senses. She notices no difference; size, form, colour, distance, are elements as real to her now as before. In respect again to the future, she sees it, but not in the sense of the annihilation of time; she foresees it; it is the future present to her; time she measures, present and future, with strange precision; strange, yet an approximation instead of this certainty would have been yet more puzzling.

So it appears that our notions of matter, force and the like, and of the conditions of space and time apart from which we can conceive nothing, are not figments to suit our human and temporary being, but elements of eternal truth.

Letter VIII
RELIGIOUS DELUSIONS

There have been occasions when much excitement on the subject of religion has prevailed, and when strange disorders of the nervous system have developed themselves among the people, which have been interpreted as immediate visitings of the holy spirit. The interpretation was delusive; the belief in it, superstition. The effects displayed were neither more nor less than phenomena of trance, the physiological consequences of the prevailing excitement. The reader will have no difficulty in identifying forms of this affection in the varieties of religious seizures, which without further comment I proceed to exemplify.

Every one will have met with allusions to some extraordinary scenes which took place in the Cevennes at the close of the seventeenth century.

It was towards the end of the year 1688 a report was first heard, of a gift of prophecy which had shown itself among the persecuted followers of the Reformation, who, in the south of France, had betaken themselves to the mountains. The first instance was said to have occurred in the family of a glass-dealer, of the name of Du Serre, well known as the most zealous Calvinist of the neighbourhood, which was a solitary spot in Dauphiné, near Mount Peyra. In the enlarging circle of enthusiasts, Gabriel Astier and Isabella Vincent made themselves first conspicuous. Isabella, a girl of sixteen years of age, from Dauphiné, who was in the service of a peasant, and tended sheep, began in her sleep to preach and prophesy, and the Reformers came from far and near to hear her. An advocate, of the name of Gerlan, describes the following scene which he had witnessed. At his request she had admitted him, and a good many others, after nightfall, to a meeting at a chateau in the neighbourhood. She there disposed herself upon a bed, shut her eyes, and went to sleep; in her sleep she chanted in a low tone the Commandments and a psalm; after a short respite she began to preach; in a louder voice, not in her own dialect, but in good French, which hitherto she had not used. The theme was an exhortation to obey God rather than man. Sometimes she spoke so quickly as to be hardly intelligible. At certain of her pauses, she stopped to collect herself. She accompanied her words with gesticulations. Gerlan found her pulse quiet, her arm not rigid, but relaxed, as natural. After an interval, her countenance put on a mocking expression, and she began anew her exhortation, which was now mixed with ironical reflections upon the Church of Rome. She then suddenly stopped, continuing asleep. It was in vain they stirred her. When her arms were lifted and let go, they dropped unconsciously. As several now went away, whom her silence rendered impatient, she said in a low tone, but just as if she was awake, "Why do you go away? Why do not you wait till I am ready?" And then she delivered another ironical discourse against the Catholic Church. She closed the scene with a prayer.

When Bouchier, the intendant of the district, heard of the performances of Isabella Vincent, he had her brought before him. She replied to his interrogatories, that people had often told her that she preached in her sleep, but that she did not herself believe a word of it. As the slightness of her person made her appear younger than she really was, the intendant merely sent her to an hospital at Grenoble; where, notwithstanding that she was visited by persons of the Reformed persuasion, there was an end of her preaching, — she became a Catholic!

Gabriel Astier, who had been a young labourer, likewise from Dauphiné, went in the capacity of a preacher and prophet into the valley of Bressac, in the Vivarais. He had infected his family: his father, mother, elder brother, and sweetheart, followed his example, and took to prophesying. Gabriel, before he preached, used to fall into a kind of stupor in which he lay rigid. After delivering his sermon, he would dismiss his auditors with a kiss, and the words: "My brother, or my sister, I impart to you the Holy Ghost." Many believed that they had thus received the Holy Ghost from Astier, being taken with the same seizure. During the period of the discourse, first one, then another, would fall down; some described themselves afterwards as having felt first a weakness and trembling through the whole frame, and an impulse to yawn and stretch their arms, then they fell convulsed and foaming at the mouth. Others carried the contagion home with them, and first experienced its effects, days, weeks, months afterwards. They believed — nor is it wonderful they did so — that they had received the Holy Ghost.

Not less curious were the seizures of the Convulsionnaires at the grave of the Abbé Paris, in the year 1727. These Jansenist visionaries used to collect in the church-yard of St. Médard, round the grave of the deposed and deceased Deacon, and before long the reputation of the place for working miracles getting about, they fell in troops into convulsions. They required, to gratify an internal impulse or feeling, that the most violent blows should be inflicted upon them at the pit of the stomach. Carré de Montgeron mentions, that being himself an enthusiast in the matter, he had inflicted the blows required with an iron instrument, weighing from twenty to thirty pounds, with a round head. And as a convulsionary lady complained that he struck too lightly to relieve the feeling of depression at her stomach, he gave her sixty blows with all his force. It would not do, and she begged to have the instrument used by a tall, strong man, who stood by in the crowd. The spasmodic tension of her muscles must have been enormous; for she received one hundred blows, delivered with such force that the wall shook behind her. She thanked the man for his benevolent aid, and contemptuously censured De Montgeron for his weakness, or want of faith and timidity. It was, indeed, time for issuing the mandate, which, as wit read it, ran:

"De par le roi — Defense à Dieu,
De faire miracle en ce lieu."

In the revivals of modern times, scenes parallel to the above have been renewed.

"I have seen," says Mr. Le Roi Sunderland, himself a preacher, (Zion's Watchman, New York, Oct. 2, 1842,) "persons often 'lose their strength,' as it is called, at camp-meetings, and other places of great religious excitement; and not pious people alone, but those also who were not professors of religion. In the spring of 1824, while performing pastoral labour in Dennis, Massachusetts, I saw more than twenty people affected in this way. Two young men, of the name of Crowell, came one day to a prayer meeting. They were quite indifferent. I conversed with them freely, but they showed no signs of penitence. From the meeting they went to their shop, (they were shoemakers,) to finish some work before going to the meeting in the evening. On seating themselves they were both struck perfectly stiff. I was immediately sent for, and found them sitting paralysed (he means cataleptic) on their benches, with their work in their hands, unable to get up, or to move at all. I have seen scores of persons affected the same way. I have seen persons lie in this state forty eight hours. At such times they are unable to converse, and are sometimes unconscious of what is passing round them. At the same time they say they are in a happy state of mind."

The following extract from the same journal portrays another kind of nervous seizure, as it was manifested at the great revival, some forty years ago, at Kentucky and Tennessee.

"The convulsions were commonly called 'the jerks.' A writer, (M'Neman,) quoted by Mr. Power, (Essay on the Influence of the Imagination over the Nervous System,) gives this account of their course and progress:—

"'At first appearance these meetings exhibited nothing to the spectator but a scene of confusion, that could scarcely be put into language. They were generally opened with a sermon, near the close of which there would be an unusual outcry, some bursting out into loud ejaculations of prayer, etc.

"'The rolling exercise consisted in being cast down in a violent manner, doubled with the head and feet together, or stretched in a prostrate manner, turning swiftly over like a dog. Nothing in nature could better represent the jerks, than for one to goad another alternately on every side with a piece of red-hot iron. The exercise commonly began in the head, which would fly backwards and forwards, and from side to side, with a quick jolt, which the person would naturally labour to suppress, but in vain. He must necessarily go on as he was stimulated, whether with a violent dash on the ground, and bounce from place to place, like a foot-ball; or hopping round with head, limbs and trunk, twitching and jolting in every direction, as if they must inevitably fly asunder; etc."

The following sketch is from Dow's journal. In the year 1805 he preached at Knoxville, Tennessee, before the governor, when some hundred and fifty persons among whom were a number of Quakers had the jerks. "I have seen,' says the writer, "all denominations of religions exercized by the jerks, gentleman and lady, black and white, young and old, without exception. I passed a meeting-house, where I observed the undergrowth had been cut down for camp-meetings, and from fifty to a hundred saplings were left for the people who were jerked to hold by. I observed, where they had held on they had kicked up the earth, as a horse stamping flies."

A widely different picture to the above is given in a letter from the Earl of Shrewsbury to A. M. Phillips Esq., published in 1841, and describing the state of two "religieuses," who were visited by members of their own communion in the belief that they lay in a sort of heavenly beatitude. To this idea their stillness, the devotional attitude of their hands and expression of their countenances, together with their manifestation of miraculous intuition contributed. But I am afraid that to the eye of a physician their condition would have been simple trance. However while one regrets the absence of reasonable enlightenment in the display, one agreeably recognizes the influence of the humanity of modern times. Had these young women lived two centuries ago, they would have been the subjects of other discipline, and their history had I possessed it to quote, must have been transferred to the darker section, which I have next to enter on.

The belief in possession by devils, which existed in the middle ages and subsequently, embraced several dissimilar cases. The first of them, which I will exemplify would have included individuals in the state of the "religieuses" described by Lord Shrewsbury. Behaviour and powers, which the people could not understand, even if exhibited by good and virtuous persons, and only expressive of or used for right purposes, were construed into the operation of unholy influences. The times were the reign of terror in religion. I give the following instance. Marie Bucaille, a native of normandy, became towards the year 1700, the subject of fits which ordinarily lasted three or four hours. It appears by the depositions of persons of character on her trial, that Marie had effected many cures seemingly by her prayers; that she comprehended and executed directions given to her mentally; that she read the thoughts of others. When in the fit the Curé of Golleville placed in the hands of Marie a folded note. Without opening the note she replied to the questions which it contained; and without knowing the writer she accurately described her person. Altho' Marie only employed her powers to cure the sick and in the service of religion, she was not the less condemned to death by the parliament of Valogne. The parliament of Rouen mitigated her punishment to whipping and public ignominy.

A second class who came nearer to the exact idea of being possessed by devils, were persons who were deranged, and entertained something of that impression themselves, and avowed it. I am not speaking of single instances; but of an extensive popular delusion, or frenzy rather, which prevailed in the fifteenth and sixteenth centuries in parts of Europe as an epidemic seizure. It was called the wolf-sickness. Those affected betook themselves to the forests as wild-beasts. One of these, who was brought before De Lancre at Bordeaux in the beginning of the sixteenth century, was a young man of Besançon. He avowed himself to be huntsman of the forest lord, his invisible master. He believed that through the power of his master, he had been transformed into a wolf; that he hunted in the forest as such; and that he was often accompanied by a bigger wolf, whom he suspected to be the master he served; with more details of the same kind. The persons thus affected were called Wehrwolves. Their common fate was the alternative of recovering from their derangement, under the influence of exorcism and its accessories, or of being executed.

The third and proper type of possession by devils presented more complicated features. The patient's state was not uniform. Often or for the most part his appearance and behaviour were natural; — then paroxysms would supervene, in which he appeared fierce, malignant, demoniacal; in which he believed himself to be possessed and acted up to the character; or if it were a lady, there might be rather the expression of suffering, with a mysterious altered manner; in both cases manifestations of superhuman knowledge. The explanation of these features is happily given by Dr. Fischer of Basle, author of an excellent work on somnambulism. He resolves them with evident justice into recurrent fits of trance, the patient when entranced being at the same time deranged; and he exemplifies his hypothesis by the case of a german lady who had fits of trance, in which she fancied herself a french emigrèe; it would have been as easy for her, had it been the mode, to have fancied herself, and to have played the part of being, possessed by the fiend. The case is this.

Gmelin, in the first volume of his Contributions to Anthropology, narrates, that in the year 1789, a German lady, under his observation, had daily paroxysms, in which she believed herself to be, and acted the part of a French emigrant. She had been in distress of mind through the absence of a person she was attached to, and he was somehow implicated in the scenes of the French revolution. After an attack of fever and delirium, the complaint regulated itself, and took the form of a daily fit of trance-waking. When the time for the fit approached, she stopped in her conversation, and ceased to answer when spoken to; she then remained a few minutes sitting perfectly still, her eyes fixed on the carpet before her. Then, in evident uneasiness, she began to move her head backwards and forwards, to sigh, and to pass her fingers across her eyebrows. This lasted a minute; then she raised her eyes, looked once or twice around with timidity and embarrassment, then began to talk in French; when she would describe all the particulars of her escape from France, and, assuming the manner of a French woman, talk purer and better accented French than she had been known to be capable of talking before, correct her friends when they spoke incorrectly, but delicately and with a comment on the German rudeness of laughing at the bad pronunciation of strangers; and if led herself to speak or read German, she used a French accent, and spoke it ill; and the like.

We have by this time had intercourse enough with spirits and demons to prepare us for the final subject of witchcraft.

The superstition of witchcraft stretches back into remote antiquity, and has many roots. In Europe it is partly of Druidical origin. The Druidesses were part priestesses, part shrewd old ladies, who dealt in magic and medicine. They were called allrune, all-knowing. There was some touch of classical superstition mingled in the stream which was flowing down to us, — so an edict of a council of Trêves, in the year 1310, has this injunction: "Nulla mulierum se nocturnis horis equitare cum Dianâ profiteatur; hæc enim dœmoniaca est illusio." But the main source from which we derived this superstition, is the East, and traditions and facts incorporated in our religion. There were only wanted the ferment of thought of the fifteenth century, the energy, ignorance, enthusiasm, and faith of those days, and the papal denunciation of witchcraft by the Bull of Innocent the VIII. in 1459, to give fury to the delusion. And from this time for three centuries, the flames, at which more than 100,000 victims perished, cast a lurid light over Europe.

But the fires are out; the superstition is extinct; and its history is trite and has lost all interest; so I will hasten to the one point in it, which deserves, which indeed requires, explanation. I do not advert to the late duration of the belief in witchcraft; so late, that it is but a century this very month of January since the last witch, a lady and a subprioress, whose confession I will afterwards give, was executed in germany; while at the same period a strong effort was made in Scotland by good and conscientious and otherwise sensible persons to reanimate the embers of the delusion, as is shewn by the following evidence. In February 1743 the associate presbytery meaning the presbytery of the secession or seceders (from the scottish established church) passed and soon thereafter published an act for renewing the national covenant; in which there is a solemn acknowledgment of sins and vow to renounce them; among which sins is specified "the repeal of the penal statutes against witchcraft contrary to the express laws of God, and for which a holy God may be provoked, in a way of righteous judgement to leave those who are already ensnared to be hardened more and more and to permit Satan to tempt and seduce others to the same wicked and dangerous snare." (note Edin. Rev. Jan. 1847.) Nor is the marvel in the absolute belief of the people in witchcraft only two centuries ago; what could they do but believe, when the witches and sorcerers themselves before their execution often avowed their guilt; and told how they had laid themselves out to league with the evil spirit; how they had gone through a regular process of initiation in the black art; how they had been rebaptised with the support of regular witch-sponsors; how they had abjured Christ, and had entered to the best of their belief into a compact with the devil; and had commenced accordingly a suitable course of bad works, poisoning and bewitching men and cattle, and the like.

Nor is the marvel in the unfairness with which those accused of witchcraft were treated. So at Lindheim Horst reports on one occasion six women were implicated in a charge of having disinterred the body of a child to make a witchbroth. As they happened to be innocent of the deed, they underwent the most cruel tortures before they would confess it. At length they saw their cheapest bargain was to admit the crime, and be simply burned alive and have it over. They did so. But the husband of one of them procured an official examination of the grave; when the child's body was found in its coffin safe and sound. What said the Inquisitor? "This is indeed a proper piece of devil's work; no, no, I am not to be taken in by such a gross and obvious imposture. Luckily the women have already confessed the crime, and burned they must and shall be in honour of the Holy Trinity, which has commanded the extirpation of sorcerers and witches." The six women were burned alive accordingly. For the people had fits of frenzied terror, which required to be allayed by the sacrifice of a victim or two. And justice became confused, to be sure in those days her head was never very clear, and threw by mistake the odium of the crime into the accusing scale; the other flew up significantly of the full extent to which mercy could interfere to temper the law. A curious instance of an epidemic attack of the belief in witchcraft occurred at Salzburg between the years 1627 and 1629, originating in a sickness among the cattle in the neighbourhood. The sickness was unluckily attributed to witchcraft, and an active inquiry was set on foot to detect the participators in the crime. It was very successful; for we find in the list of persons burned alive on this occasion, besides children of 14, 12, 11, 10, 9 years of age, fourteen canons, four gentlemen of the choir, two young men of rank, a fat old lady of rank, the wife of a burgomaster, a counsellor, the fattest burgess of Würzburg, together with his wife the handsomest woman in the city, and a midwife of the name of Shickelte, with whom (according to a N. B. in the original raport) the whole of the mischief originated.

The marvel in witchcraft is the belief entertained by the sorcerers and witches themselves of its reality. That many of these persons, shrewd and unprincipled, should have practised for gain on the credulity of others and pretended to rely on their art is conceivable, and only what is still occasionally done in modern times. But that they should, as it is proved by some of their confessions previously to execution, have themselves been convinced of the reality of their intercourse with the devil, is surprizing enough to deserve explanation. A single crucial instance will bring us upon the trail of the solution.

A little maid, twelve years of age used to fall into fits of sleep; and afterwards she told her parents and the judge, how an old woman and her daughter, riding on a broom-stick, had come and taken her out with them. The daughter sat foremost, the old woman behind, the little maid between. They went away through the roof of the house, over the adjoining houses and the towngate, to a village some way off. Upon arriving there the party went down the chimney of a cottage into a room, where sat a black man and twelve women. They eat and drank. The black man filled their glasses from a cann, and gave each of the women a handful of gold. She herself had received none, but she had eaten and drank with them.

See how much this example displays. I mean, not that the superstition was imbibed in childhood, tho' that would do much to establish the belief in it, — but that it had power to disturb the mind sufficiently to produce trance-sleep; for such were evidently the fits of sleep this child described; and trance-sleep with its special character of visions, of dreams vivid, coherent, continuous, realizing the ideas, which had driven the mind into trance. Elder persons, it is to be presumed, were occasionally similarly wrought upon. And the witches seemed to have known and availed themselves of the confidence in their art that could be thus promoted; and by witch-broths, of which narcotics formed an ingredient, they would induce in themselves and in their pupils a heavy stupor, which so far resembles trance, that vivid and connected dreams occur in it. Here was the seeming reality necessary for absolute belief. It lay in not-understood trance-phenomena. Other evidence from the same source came in to support the first. Some of the witch-pupils in their trances would shew a strange knowledge; some of the victims, on whose fears or persons they had wrought, would become possessed; proving their art to be not less real, than they believed thus the elementary part to be of their personal communication with the fiend. These remarks explain collaterally why witches and sorceresses were more numerous than sorcerers and magicians. Insufficient occupation and other causes helped probably to dispose women to seek a resource in the intense excitement of this crime; but besides, trance stood at their service, which men seldomer experience.

I will conclude with two pictures; one the confession, interesting however from its relation to the child's early vision, of vulgar and ordinary witches; — the other the substance of the confession of a lady-witch, which in itself tells the whole curious tale of this disease.

At Mora, in Sweden, in 1669, of many who were put to the torture and executed, seventy-two women agreed in the following avowal — That they were in the habit of meeting at a place called Blocula. That on their calling out "Come forth," the Devil used to appear to them in a gray coat, red breeches, gray stockings, with a red beard, and a peaked hat with party-coloured feathers on his head. He then enforced upon them, not without blows, that they must bring him, at nights, their own and other peoples' children, stolen for the purpose. They travel through the air to Blocula either on beasts or on spits, or broomsticks. When they have many children with them, they rig on an additional spar to lengthen the back of the goat or their broom-stick that the children may have room to sit. At Blocula they sign their name in blood and are baptized. The Devil is a humorous, pleasant gentleman; but his table is coarse enough, which makes the children often sick on their way home, the product being the socalled witch-butter found in the fields. When the Devil is larky, he solicits the witches to dance round him on their brooms, which he suddenly pulls from under them, and uses to beat them with till they are black and blue. He laughs at this joke till his sides shake again. Sometimes he is in a more gracious mood, and plays to them lovely airs upon the harp; and occasionally sons and daughters are born to the Devil, which take up their residence at Blocula.

The following is the history of the lady-witch. She was, at the time of her death, seventy years of age, and had been many years sub-prioress of the convent of Unterzell, near Würtzburg.

Maria Renata took the veil at nineteen years of age, against her inclination, having previously been initiated in the mysteries of witchcraft, which she continued to practise for fifty years under the cloak of punctual attendance to discipline and pretended piety. She was long in the station of sub-prioress, and would, for her capacity, have been promoted to the rank of prioress, had she not betrayed a certain discontent with the ecclesiastic life, a certain contrariety to her superiors, something half expressed only of inward dissatisfaction. Renata had not ventured to let any one about the convent into her confidence, and she remained free from suspicion, notwithstanding that, from time to time, some of the nuns, either from the herbs she mixed with their food, or through sympathy, had strange seizures, of which some died. Renata became at length extravagant and unguarded in her witch-propensities, partly from long security, partly from desire of stronger excitement; made noises in the dormitory, and uttered shrieks in the garden; went at nights into the cells of the nuns to pinch and torment them, to assist her in which she kept a considerable supply of cats. The removal of the keys of the cells counteracted this annoyance; but a still more efficient means was a determined blow on the part of a nun, struck at the aggressor with the penitential scourge one night, on the morning following which Renata was observed to have a black eye and cut face. This event awakened suspicion against Renata. Then, one of the nuns, who was much esteemed, declared, believing herself upon her death-bed, that, "as she shortly expected to stand before her Maker, Renata was uncanny, that she had often at nights been visibly tormented by her, and that she warned her to desist from this course." General alarm arose, and apprehension of Renata's arts; and one of the nuns, who previously had had fits, now became possessed, and in the paroxysms told the wildest tales against Renata. It is only wonderful how the sub-prioress contrived to keep her ground many years against these suspicions and incriminations. She adroitly put aside the insinuations of the nun as imaginary or of calumnious intention, and treated witchcraft and possession of the Devil as things which enlightened people no longer believed in. As, however, five more of the nuns, either taking the infection from the first, or influenced by the arts of Renata, became possessed of devils and unanimously attacked Renata, the superiors could no longer avoid making a serious investigation of the charges. Renata was confined in a cell alone, whereupon the six devils screeched in chorus at being deprived of their friend. She had begged to be allowed to take her papers with her; but this being refused, and thinking herself detected, she at once avowed to her confessor and the superiors, that she was a witch, had learned witchcraft out of the convent, and had bewitched the six nuns. They determined to keep the matter secret, and to attempt the conversion of Renata. And as the nuns still continued possessed, they despatched her to a remote convent. Here, under a show of outward piety, she still went on with her attempts to realise witchcraft, and the nuns remained possessed. It was decided at length to give Renata over to the civil power. She was accordingly condemned to be burned alive; but in mitigation of punishment her head was first struck off. Four of the possessed nuns gradually recovered, with clerical assistance; the other two remained deranged. Renata was executed on the 21ˢᵗ January 1749.

Renata stated, in her voluntary confession, that she had often at night been carried bodily to witch-Sabbaths; in one of which she was first presented to the Prince of Darkness, when she abjured God and the Virgin at the same time. Her name, with the alteration of Maria into Emma, was written in a black book, and she herself was stamped on the back as the Devil's property; in return for which she received the promise of seventy years of life and of all she might wish for. She stated that she had often, at night, gone into the cellar of the chateau and drank the best wine; in the shape of a swine had walked on the convent walls; on the bridge had milked the cows as they passed over; and several times had mingled with the actors in the theatre in London.

Letter IX
MESMERISM

The powers, which we have seen successfully employed to shake the nerves and unsettle the mind in the service of superstition, can they be turned to no useful purpose?

A satisfactory answer to the question may be found in the invention of ether-inhalation and in the history of mesmerism. The witch narcotized her pupils in order to produce in them delusive visions; the surgeon stupefies his patient to annul the pain of an operation. The fanatic preacher excites convulsions and trance in his auditory as evidence of the workings of the holy spirit; Mesmer produced the same effects in his patients as a means of curing disease.

It occurred to Mr. Jackson, a chemist of the united states, that it might be possible harmlessly to stupefy a patient through the inhalation of the vapor of sulphuric ether, to such an extent that a surgical operation would be unfelt by him. He communicated the idea to Mr. Morton, a dentist, who carried it into execution with the happiest results. The patient became insensible; a tooth was extracted; no pain seemed felt at the time; no ill consequence followed. Led by the report of this success, in the course of the autumn of 1846, Messrs. Bigelow, Warren, and Heywood, ventured to employ the same means in surgical operations of a more serious description. The results obtained on these occasions were not less satisfactory than the first had been. Since then, in England, France, and Germany, the same interesting experiment has been repeated many hundred times, and the adoption of this or of a parallel method has become general in surgery.

I withdraw from the present letter a sketch which I had made from the "report" of Dr. Heyfelder, of the phenomena of etherisation. For, a year had barely elapsed, when the narcotizing agent recommended by Mr. Jackson was superseded by another, suggested and brought into use by Professor Simpson of Edinburgh. The inhalation of chloroform is found to be more rapid and uniform and certain in its effects, and compassable in a simpler manner, than the inhalation of ether. Its brief phenomena are wound up by the production of stupor; they are remotely comparable to those produced by alkohol. It is perhaps questionable whether the process is as safe as etherisation. But the time is passed when I enjoyed the means of looking through and forming a practical judgment upon discoveries like the present. Not the less however do I hail the advent of this as a boon to the art of surgery. The conception was original, bold, and reasonable; its execution neat and scientific; its success wonderful. It established in the year 1847 to the satisfaction of the public and of the medical profession, that the exclusion of pain from surgical operations is a practicable idea and the attempt to realize it a legitimate pursuit.

Then what is Mesmerism?

The object of the inventor of the art was to cure diseases through the influence of a new force brought by him to bear upon the human frame.

Talent, for philosophy or business, is the power of seeing what is yet hidden from others. As the eyes of some animals are fitted to see best in the dark; so the mental vision of some original minds prefers exercizing itself on obscure and occult subjects. Whoever indulges this turn will certainly pass for a charlatan; most likely he will prove one. Mesmer had it, and indulged it, in a high degree. The body of science which I have unfolded in the preceding letters was wholly unknown in his time (he was born in 1734); but he was led by his wayward instinct to grope after it in the dark, and he seized and brought to upper light fragmentary elements of strange capabilities, which he strove to interpret and to use. He had early displayed a bias towards the mystical. When a student at Vienna, (he was by birth a swiss) his principal study was astrology. He sought in the stars a force, which extending throughout space, might influence the beings living upon our planet. In the year 1766 he published his lucabrations. In attempting to identify his imaginary force Mesmer first supposed it to be electricity. Afterwards about the year 1773 he adopted the idea that it must be magnetism. So at Vienna, from 1773 to 1775 he employed the practice of stroking diseased parts of the body with magnets. But in 1776 happening to be upon a tour, he fell in with a mystical monk of the name of Gassner, who was then occupied in curing the prince-bishop of Ratisbon of blindness by exorcism. Then Mesmer observed that without using magnets Gassner produced much the same effects on the living body, which he had produced with them. The fact was not lost upon him; he threw aside his magnets, and operated mostly afterwards with the hand alone. It appears that he was often successful in curing disease; or that his patients not only experienced sensible effects from his proceedures, but frequently recovered from their complaints. But in 1777, his reputation, which must have always hung upon a very slender thread, broke down through a failure in the case of the musician Paradies. So Mesmer left Vienna, and in the following year betook himself to Paris. There he obtained a success, which quickly drew upon him the indignation, perhaps the jealousy of the faculty, who failed not to stigmatize him as a charlatan. They exclaimed against him for practising an art, which he would not divulge; and when he offered to display it, averred that he threw difficulties in the way of their investigations; perhaps he suspected them of want of fairness in their inquiries; perhaps he was really unwilling to part with his secret; he refused an offer from the government of 20,000 francs if he would disclose it; but he communicated freely to individuals under a pledge of secrecy all he knew for a hundred louis. His practice itself gave most support to the allegation against him. His patients were received with an air of mystery and studied effect. The apartment hung with mirrors was dimly lighted. A profound silence was observed, broken only by strains of music which occasionally floated through the rooms. The patients were seated round a sort of vat, which contained a heterogeneous mixture of chemical ingredients. With this and with each other they were placed in relation by means of cords or jointed rods, or by holding hands; and among them slowly and mysteriously moved Mesmer himself, affecting one by a touch, another by a look, a third by passes with his hand, a fourth by pointing with a rod.

What followed is easily conceivable from the scenes referred to in my last letter as witnessed at religions revivals. One person became hysterical, then another; one was seized with catalepsy; others with convulsions; some with palpitations of the heart, perspirations, and other bodily disturbances. These effects, however various and different, went all by the name of "salutary crises." The method was supposed to provoke in the sick person exactly the kind of action propitious to his recovery. And it may easily be imagined that many a patient found himself the better after a course of this rude empiricism; and that the effect made by these events passing daily in Paris must have been very considerable. To the ignorant the scene was full of wonderment.

To ourselves, regarding it from our present vantage-ground, it presents no marvellous characters. The phenomena were the same which we have been recently contemplating, — a group of disorders of the nervous system. The causes which were present are not less familiar to us, nor their capability of producing such effects; they were — mental excitement, here consisting in raised expectation and fear; — the contagiousness of hysteria, convulsions, and trance, its force increased by the numbers and close packing of the patients; — the

Od force, developed by the chemical action in the charged cauldron, developed by each of the excited bodies around, its action first favored by the absolute stillness observed, then by the increasing sensibility of the patients as their nerves became more and more shaken. It is remarkable that Jussieu, — the most competent judge in the commission of inquiry into the truth of mesmerism set on foot at Paris in 1784, of which Franklin was a member, and which condemned mesmerism as an imposture, — was so struck with what he saw that he strongly recommended the subject to the attention and study of physicians. His objections were against the theory alone. He laid it down in the separate report, which he gave in, that no physical cause had been proved to be in operation beyond animal heat! curiously overlooking the fact that common heat would not produce the effects observed; and therefore that the latter must have been owing to that something which animal heat, or the radiating warmth of a living body, contains, in addition to common heat. That something we now know, but only since 1845, to be the Od force.

The Od force is so new, so young in science, that Mesmer's reputation has not yet been credited with the honor thence reflected upon it. I will not say that Mesmer's astral force was a distinct anticipation of von Reichenbach's discovery, which was no ways suggested by the former, and was from first to last an effort of inductive observation. But the guess of the mystic had certainly a most happy parallelism to the truth, which a different sort of mind tracked in the same field. For the Od force reaches us even from the stars, and the sun and the fixed stars are Od-negative; and the planets and the moon, Od-positive. I read in the newspaper that Dr. Faraday has seen indications of a new polar force in certain crystals; it may possibly prove the same with von Reichenbach's Od. It is unnecessary to follow Mesmer through his minor performances. The relief sometimes obtained by stroking diseased parts with the hand — that is, the effects obtained through the local action of Od — had been before proclaimed by Dr. Greatrex, whose pretensions had had no less an advocate than the Honble Robert Boyle. The extraordinary tales of Mesmer's personal power over individuals are probably part exaggeration, part real results of his confidence and skill in the use of the means he wielded. Mesmer died in 1815.

Among his pupils, when at the zenith of his fame, was the Marquis de Puységur. Returning from serving at the siege of Gibraltar, this young officer found mesmerism the mode at Paris, and appears to have become for no other reason one of the initiated. At the end of a course of instruction, he professed himself to be no wiser than when it began; and he ridiculed the credulity of his brothers, who were staunch adherents of the new doctrine. However he did not forget his lesson; and on going the same spring to his estate at Besancy, near Soissons, he took occasion to mesmerize the daughter of his agent and another young person, for the tooth-ache, and they declared themselves, in a few minutes, cured. This questionable success was sufficient to lead M. de Puységur, a few days after, to try his hand on a young peasant of the name of Victor, who was suffering with a severe fluxion on his chest. What was M. de Puységur's surprize, when, at the end of a few minutes, Victor went off into a kind of tranquil sleep, without crisis or convulsion, and in that sleep began to gesticulate, and talk, and enter into his private affairs. Then he became sad; and M. de Puységur tried mentally to inspire him with cheerful thoughts; he hummed a lively tune to himself, inaudibly, and immediately Victor began to sing the air. Victor remained asleep for an hour, and awoke composed, with his symptoms mitigated.

The case of Victor revolutionized the art of Mesmerism. The large part of his life, in which M. de Puységur had nothing to do but to follow this vein of inquiry, was occupied in practising and advocating a gentle manipulation to produce sleep, in preference to the more exciting means which led to the violent crises in Mesmer's art. I have no plea for telling how M. de Puységur served in the first french revolutionary armies; how he quitted the service in disgust; how narrowly he escaped the guillotine; how he lived in retirement afterwards; benevolently endeavouring to do good to his sick neighbours by means of mesmerism; how he survived the restoration; and how finally he died of a cold caught by serving in the encampment at Rheims at the coronation of Charles X.

For he had fulfilled his mission the day that he put Victor to sleep. He had made a vast stride in advance of his teacher. Not but that Mesmer must frequently have induced the same condition; but he had passed it by unheeded as one only of numerous equivalent forms of salutary crises: or that M. de Puységur himself estimated, or had the means of estimating, the real nature and value of the step which he had made. To himself he appeared to be winning a larger domain for mesmerism, when in fact he had emerged into an independent field, into which mesmerism happened to have a gate.

The state, which he had induced in Victor, was common trance, the initiatory sleep, followed by half-waking. He had obtained this result by using the Od force with quietness and gentleness; leaving out the exciting mental agencies, to which the mixture of violent seizures in Mesmer's practice is attributable. The gentler method has been adopted and practised by the successors of M. de Puységur, by Deleuze, Bertrand, Georget, Rostan, Foissac, Elliotson, and others. To Dr. Elliotson, the most successful probably, certainly the most scientific employer of the practice of Mesmerism, the credit is due of having introduced its use into England; the credit, — for it required no little moral courage to encounter the storm of opposition, with which his honest zeal in the advocacy of an unpopular practical truth was met. It is but fair to add, that tho' his theory has been superseded, and his method changed, to Mesmer belongs the merit of having first tracked out and realized this path of discovery. The golden medal is his.

The modern practice of Mesmerism contemplates two objects; one, the application of the Od force to produce local effects; the other its employment to induce trance. In the present slight sketch I shall say nothing on the first subject; but let me describe how trance is induced. It is to be observed that attention to certain conditions favors very much the success of the experiment. The room should not be too light; very few persons should be present; the patient and the operator should be quiet, tranquil, composed; the patient should be fasting. The operator has then only to sit down before the patient; who is likewise sitting with his hands resting on his knees and gently closed, with the thumbs upwards. The operator then lays his hands half open upon the patient's, pressing the thumbs against those of the patient, as it were taking thumbs; this is a more convenient attitude than taking hands in the ordinary way. The operator and patient have then only to sit still. An Od-current is established; and if the patient is susceptible, he will soon become drowzy, and perhaps be entranced at the first sitting. Instead of this, the two hands of the operator may be held horizontally with the fingers pointed to the patient's forehead; and either maintained in this position, or brought downwards in frequent passes opposite to the patient's face, shoulders, arms; the points of the fingers being held as near the patient as possible without touching.

It is easy theoretically to explain the beneficial results, which follow from the daily induction of trance for an hour or so, in various forms of disorder of the nervous system, — in epilepsy, — in tic douloureux, — in nervous palsy and the like. As long as the state of trance is maintained, so long is the nervous system in a state of repose. It is more or less completely put out of gear. It experiences the same relief, which a sprained joint feels, when you dispose it in a relaxed position on a pillow. A chance is thus given to the strained nerves of recovering their tone of health. And it is wonderful how many cases of nervous disorder get well at once through these simple means. As it is certain that there is no disease, in which the nervous system is not primarily or secondarily implicated, it is impossible to foresee, what will prove the limit to the beneficial application of Mesmerism in medical practice.

In operative surgery the art is not less available. In trance the patient is insensible; and a limb may be removed without the operation exciting disturbance of any kind. And what is equally important, in all the after-treatment, at every dressing, the process of mesmerizing may be resorted to again; with no possible disadvantage, but being rather soothing and useful to the patient, independently of the extinction of the dread and suffering of pain. The first instance in which an operation was performed on a patient in this state, was the celebrated case of Madame Plantin. It occurred twenty years ago. The lady was sixty four years of age, and laboured under scirrhus of the breast. She was prepared for the operation by M. Chapélain, who on several successive days threw her into trance by the ordinary mesmeric manipulations. She was *then* like an ordinary sleep-walker, and would converse with indifference about the contemplated operation, the idea of which, when she was in her natural state, filled her with terror. The operation of removing the diseased breast was performed at Paris on the 12th of April 1829, by M. Jules Cloquet: it lasted from ten to twelve minutes. During the whole of this time, the patient *in her trance* conversed calmly with M. Cloquet, and exhibited not the slightest sign of suffering. Her expression of countenance did not change, nor were the voice, the breathing, or the pulse, at all affected. After the wound was dressed, the patient was awakened from the trance, when, on learning that the operation was over, and seeing her children round her, Madame Plantin was affected with considerable emotion, whereupon M. Chapélain, to compose her, put her back into the state of trance.

I copy the above particulars from Dr. Foissac's "*Rapports et Discussions de l'Académie Royale de Médicine sur le Magnetism animal.*" — Paris 1833. "My friend, Dr. Warren of Boston, informed me that, being at Paris, he had asked M. Jules Cloquet if the story were true. M. Cloquet answered, "Perfectly." "Then why," said Dr. Warren, "have you not repeated the practice?" M. Cloquet replied, "that he had not dared, that the prejudice against mesmerism was so strong at Paris, that he probably would have lost his reputation and his income by so doing."

It has been mentioned that in ordinary trance the mind appears to gain new powers. For a long time we had to trust to the chance-turning up of cases of spontaneous trance, in the experience of physicians of observation, for any light we could hope would be thrown on those extraordinary phenomena. Now we possess around us, on every side, adequate opportunities for completely elucidating these events, if we please to employ them. The philosopher, when his speculations suggest a new question to be put, can summon the attendance of a trance, as easily as the Jupiter of the Iliad summoned a dream. Or, looking out for two or three cases to which the induction of trance may be beneficial, the physician may have in his house subjects for perpetual reference and daily experiment.

A gentleman with whom I have long been well acquainted, for many years Chairman of the Quarter Sessions in a northern county, of which a late year he was High Sheriff, has, like M. de Puységur, amused some of his leisure hours, and benevolently done not a little good, by taking the trouble of mesmerising invalids, whom he has thus restored to health. In constant correspondence with, and occasionally having the pleasure of seeing this gentleman, I have learned from him the common course in which the new powers of the mind which belong to trance are developed under its artificial induction. The sketch which I propose to give of this subject will be taken from his descriptions, which, I should observe, tally in all essential points with what I meet with in French and German authors. The little that I have myself seen of the matter, I will mention preliminarily.

In some, instead of trance, a common fit of hysterics is produced. In others, slight headache, and a sense of weight on the eye-brows, and difficulty of raising the eyelids, supervene.

In one young woman, whom I saw mesmerized for the first time by Dupotet, nothing resulted but a sense of pricking and tingling wherever he pointed with his hand; and her arm on one or two occasions jumped in the most natural and conclusive manner, when her eyes being covered, he directed his outstretched finger to it.

A gentleman, about thirty years of age, when the mesmerizer held his outstretched hands pointed to his head, experienced no disposition to sleep; but in two or three minutes, he began to shake his head and twist his features about; at last, his head was jerked from side to side, and forwards and backwards, with a violence that looked alarming. But he said, when it was over, that the motion had not been unpleasant; that he had moved in a sort voluntarily; although he could not refrain from it. If the hands of the operator were pointed to his arm instead of his head, the same violent jerks came in it, and gradually extended to the whole body. I asked him to try to resist the influence, by holding his arm out in strong muscular tension. This had the effect of retarding the attack of the jerks, but, when it came on, it was more violent than usual.

A servant of mine, aged about twentyfive, was mesmerized by Lafontaine, for a full half hour, and, no effect appearing to be produced, I told him he might rise from the chair, and leave us. On getting up, he looked uneasy and said his arms were numb. They were perfectly paralysed from the elbows downwards, and numb to the shoulders. This was the more satisfactory, that neither the man himself, nor Lafontaine, nor the four or five spectators, expected this result. The operator triumphantly drew a pin and stuck it into the man's hand, which bled but had no feeling. Then heedlessly, to show it gave pain, Lafontaine stuck the pin into the man's thigh, whose flashing eye, and half suppressed growl, denoted that the aggression would certainly have been returned by another, had the arm which should have done it not been really powerless. However,

M. Lafontaine made peace with the man, by restoring him the use and feeling of his arms. This was done by dusting them, as it were, by quick transverse motions of his extended hands. In five minutes nothing remained of the palsy but a slight stiffness, which gradually wore off in the course of the evening.

Genuine and ordinary trance, I have seen produced by the same manipulations in from three minutes, to half an hour. The patient's eyelids have dropped, he has appeared on the point of sleeping, but he has not sunk back upon his chair; then he has continued to sit upright, — seemingly perfectly insensible to the loudest sounds, or the acutest and most startling impressions on the sense of touch. The pulse is commonly a little increased in frequency; the breathing is sometimes heavier than usual.

Occasionally, as in Victor's case, the patient quickly and spontaneously emerges from the state of trance-sleep into trance half-waking; a rapidity of development which I am persuaded occurs much more frequently among the French than with the English or Germans. English patients, especially, for the most part require a long course of education, many sittings, to have the same powers drawn out. And these are by far the most interesting cases. I will describe from Mr. Williamson's account, the course he has usually followed in developing his patient's powers, and the order in which they have manifested themselves.

On the first day, perhaps, nothing can be elicited. But after some minutes the stupor seems as it were less embarrassing to the patient, who appears less heavily slumbrous, and breathes lighter again; or it may be the reverse, particularly if the patient is epileptic; after a little, the breathing may be deeper, the state one of less composure. Pointing with the hands to the pit of the stomach, laying the hands upon the shoulders, and slowly moving them along the arms down to the hands, the whole with the utmost quietude and composure on the part of the operator, will dispel this oppression.

And the interest of the first sitting is confined to the process of awakening the patient, which is one of the most marvellous phenomena of the whole. The operator lays his two thumbs on the space between the eyebrows, and as it were vigorously smoothes or irons the eyebrows, rubbing them from within outwards, seven or eight times. Upon this, the patient probably raises his head and his eyebrows, and draws a deeper breath as if he would yawn; he is half awake, and blowing upon the eyelids, or the repetition of the previous operation, or dusting the forehead by smart transverse wavings of the hand, or blowing upon it, causes the patient's countenance to become animated; the eyelids open, he looks about him, recognises you, and begins to speak. If any feeling of heaviness remains, any weight or pain of the forehead, another repetition of the same manipulations sets all right. And yet this patient would not have been awakened, if a gun had been fired at his ear, or his arm had been cut off.

At the next sitting, or the next to that, the living statue begins to wake in its tranced life. The operator holds one hand over the opposite hand of his patient, and makes as if he would draw the patient's hand upwards, raising his own with short successive jerks, yet not too abrupt. Then the patient's hand begins to follow his; and often having ascended some inches stops in the air catochally. This fixed state is always relieved by transverse brushings with the hand, or by breathing in addition, on the rigid limb. And it is most curious to see the whole bodily frame, over which spasmodic rigidness may have crept, thus thawed joint by joint. Then the first effect shown commonly is this motion, the patient's hand following the operator's. At the same sitting, he begins to hear, and there is intelligence in his countenance, when the operator pronounces his name; perhaps his lips move, and he begins to answer pertinently as in ordinary sleep-walking. But he hears the operator alone best, and him even in a whisper. *Your* voice, if you shout, he does not hear: unless you take the operator's hand, and then he hears *you* too. In general, however, now, the proximity of others seems in some way to be sensible to him; and he appears uneasy when they crowd close upon him. It seems that the force of the relation between the operator and his patient naturally goes on increasing, as the powers of the sleep-waker are developed; but that this is not necessarily the case, and depends upon its being encouraged by much commerce between them, and the exclusion of others from joining in this trance-communion.

And now the patient — beginning to wake in trance, hearing and answering the questions of the operator, moving each limb, or rising even, as the operator's hand is raised to draw him into obedient following — enters into a new relation with his mesmeriser. He *adopts sympathetically every voluntary movement of the other*. When the latter rises from his chair, *he* rises; when he sits down, *he* sits down; if he bows, *he* bows; if he make a grimace, *he* makes the same. Yet his eyes are closed. He certainly does not see. His mind has interpenetrated to a small extent the nervous system of the operator; and is in relation with his voluntary nerves and the anterior half of his cranio-spinal chord. (These are the organs by which the impulse to voluntary motion is conveyed and originated.) Further into the other's being, he has not yet got. So he does not *what the other thinks of, or wishes him to do;* but only what the other either does, or goes through the mental part of doing. So Victor sang the air, which M. de Puységur only mentally hummed.

The next strange phenomenon marks that the mind of the entranced patient has interpenetrated the nervous system of the other *a step farther*, and is in relation besides with the posterior half of the cranio-spinal chord and its nerves. For now the entranced person, who has no feeling, or taste, or smell of his own, *feels, tastes, and smells every thing that is made to tell on the senses of the operator.* If mustard or sugar be put in his own mouth, he seems not to know that they are there; if mustard is placed on the tongue of the operator, the entranced person expresses great disgust, and tries as if to spit it out. The same with bodily pain. If you pluck a hair from the operator's head, the other complains of the pain you give *him*.

To state in the closest way what has happened — the phenomena of sympathetic motion and sympathetic sensation, thus displayed, are exactly such as might be expected to follow, if the mind or conscious principle of the entranced person were brought into relation with the cranio-spinal chord of the operator and its nerves, and with no farther portion of his nervous system. Later, it will be seen, the interpenetration can extend farther.

But before this happens, a new phenomenon manifests itself, not of a sympathetic character. The operator contrives to wake the entranced person to the knowledge that he possesses new faculties. *He develops in him new organs of sensation,* or rather helps to hasten his recognition of their possession.

It is to be observed however, that several who can be entranced, cannot be brought as far as the present step. Others make a tantalizing half-advance towards

10

reaching it *thus*, and then stop. They are asked "do you see any thing?" After some days at length they answer, "yes." — "What?" "A light." "Where is the light?" then they intimate its place to be either before them, or to one side, or above, or behind them. And they describe the colour of the light which is commonly yellowish. And each day it is pointed to in the same direction, and is seen equally whether the room be light or dark. Their eyes in the mean time are closed. And here with many the phenomenon stops. Others in this light now begin to discern objects held in the direction in which they see it. The range of this new visual organ and the conditions under which it acts are different in different instances. Sometimes the object must be close, sometimes it is best seen at a short distance. But seen it is. The following experiment which is decisive was made at my suggestion. A gentleman standing behind the entranced person held behind him a pack of cards, from which he drew several in succession, and without seeing them himself, presented them to the new visual organ of the patient. In each case she named the card right. The degree of light suited to this new mode of vision is variable; sometimes bright daylight is best; sometimes they prefer a moderate light. Some distinguish figure and colour when the room is so dark that the bystanders can distinguish neither.

These observations, which are, however, only in conformity with similar evidence from many other quarters, I give on the authority of Mr. J. W. Williamson of Whickham, the gentleman, to whom I before alluded. The following accidental features attending the manifestation of transposed senses were further observed by Mr. Williamson.

In most of the persons, in whom Mr. Williamson has brought out transposed vision, the faculty has been located in a small surface of the scalp behind the left ear; and to see objects well the patient has held them at the distance of five or six inches from and opposite to this spot. One young woman, who had been temporarily set aside under affliction for the loss of a relative, on the experiments being resumed, saw from all parts of the head, but confusedly, a broken and incomplete picture. On a subsequent day she saw with the right side of her head. Afterwards the visual sense returned to its first place.

In one young person the new sentient organ was on the top of her head, and to see objects she required them to be brought into contact with it. Once that she had a rheumatic cold and tenderness of the scalp, she said, when entranced, putting her hand to the crown of her head, that the cold had made her eyes sore.

One person saw objects best when placed behind her at the distance of seven or eight feet.

The governess in a neighbouring family was mesmerized for tic douloureux. In seven sittings she was cured. At the second sitting in her trance she exhibited displaced sensation. She could read with her fingers ends; her way was to hold the book open against her chest, the back of the book towards her, with one hand; then she passed a finger of the other hand slowly over each word to read it.

The part-physical character of these phenomena is shewn by an observation of Dr. Petetin's on the first of his cataleptic patients. At the time that the patient heard with the pit of her stomach, he found that if with the fingers of one, say the left, hand he touched the pit of her stomach, and whispered to the fingers of his right hand, the patient heard him. But if the left hand was removed to the smallest possible distance from the patient, the contact being interrupted, she no longer heard him. Then he made a chain of seven persons, holding each others hands; the nearest to the patient was her sister, who touched the pit of her stomach; at the other end was Dr. Petetin, who whispered to his fingers, and was heard. A cane was then introduced as part of the circuit, the patient still heard. But if a stick of sealing wax or a glass rod was substituted for it, or if one of the party wore silk gloves, the patient could no longer hear Dr. Petetin. Without close observation, what is physical in the phenomena, which have thus engaged us, is liable to be overlooked; and the bystander may class them as examples of lucidity, which they are not. Organic cooperation may be traced in them all. Thus, among Mr. Williamson's earlier experiments, he tried, sitting before the entranced person, (who had shewn no lucidity) by imaging strongly to himself a white horse to force the image into her mind. When, being awakened, she had left the room, on her way she said to her fellow-servant; "what was it master said to me about a white horse? I am sure he said something." Mr. Williamson on learning the maid's remark supposed his mental operation had been successful. But the same experiment, when repeated, mostly failed. At last he found out why: It only succeeded, when in his mental urgency, he half made in his own throat the motions of the sounds that expressed the mental image. Then and then only the patient caught it. For her mind could not read his thoughts, but yet had penetrated the inferior part of the nervous system only, — the craniospinal cord; and being there, had adopted sympathetically the voluntarily impulses that were there performed; so she half moved the muscles of her own vocal organs to express the idea, and from that, its imperfect expression, received it into her thoughts. No doubt the phenomenon of Victor's singing the words to M. de Puységur's mentally hummed air was the same with the above, and not one of mesmeric lucidity, the subject which we are now approaching.

But I pause; — and go no further.

For my object in these letters generally has been to establish principles. And the phenomena of lucidity developed in artificial trance have been only the same as, and have not been as yet made more of than, the lucidity of catalepsy. No further principle has yet emerged from their study. And my special object in this letter has been to persuade the opponents of Mesmerism to do it justice; and I think I am most likely to attain my end by not attempting to prove too much.

So that nothing remains for me to do, but to observe the form, in which these letters were originally shaped, in recollection of the pleasant hours which the residence of your family at Boppard during the winter of 1844—45, caused me, and to say finally,

Dear Archy, farewell.

Postscript

A postscript is said generally to contain the pith of a letter. It is an old saw and therefore entitled to my respect; so on this occasion I will make it true.

There have been for many years persons in Paris, who gain a livelihood by their performances when entranced. The most celebrated among these persons at present is M. Alexis. A friend and patient of mine, a gentleman educated to the bar, who is passing the present winter at Paris, took occasion recently to consult M. Alexis about his health. The opinion, which M. Alexis delivered, when entranced, on the case, is more precise and minute than I had ventured to express; but it agrees with all that I had observed, and I see no reason why it should not be strictly exact. The treatment, which M. Alexis has recommended, does not differ at all from that which any medical man of experience might reasonably have ordered in such a case. I have known other instances in which the intuition of entranced persons has furnished them with a seemingly equally accurate knowledge of the complaints of persons either brought into their presence, or otherwise into relation with them. The prescriptions of persons in lucid trance seem to me mostly shrewd guesses founded upon the nature of the case and what is popularly known of the action of remedies. Sometimes, however, particularly when mesmerism or loss of blood are advised, the performers seem to have an extraordinary sagacity in measuring the dose of the remedy.

When the consultation was over, my friend asked M. Alexis a variety of questions from a list which I had sent to him. The following are the answers given to some of them.

God is every where. The human soul is a distinct principle; which when death occurs becomes separated from the body. During life the soul is imprisoned in the body. The moon is not inhabited. The planets, that are not too near to or too remote from the sun, have inhabitants; who are intelligent like man; but their degree of intelligence is much inferior to that of man.

A wild jumble this one would say of solemn truisms and of mere fudge! Certainly such a statement coming from a single entranced person is good for nothing. But suppose many persons in lucid trance of different ages, occupations, sexes, and living in different parts of the world, shall agree in the whole or in certain parts of such a story, what shall we say? the same persons proving at the same time capable of describing accurately what is taking place at two or three hundred miles distance?

My friend then put into the hand of M. Alexis my note, and asked him if he could tell him any thing about the writer. It was then half past eleven in the forenoon.

M. Alexis said "the writer is bald; short in stature, something above fifty years of age; has lost the use of his legs; he is in bed; he has a very active mind; he is a physician." Each shot hit the mark. "He lives on the sea-coast;" this my friend denied. "No" said M. Alexis on reflection, "it is not the sea but a river. He lives on the banks of the Rhine about twenty leagues from Frankfort." The bull's eye again.

My friend then asked as I had begged him to do how he got so see these things. M. Alexis said it was by an exercize of the will. That one day, however, he could see one class of things only; another day another class; and that his perception was clearer some days than others. By his will I conclude that M. Alexis meant an effort of attention. I suppose that when in this state, vistas as it were open to the seer into indefinite remoteness, and he just bends his observation to what is thus opened to him. M. Alexis said, that in conceiving a remote scene, he does not perceive what intervenes; but only the single group of things to which his attention has been drawn. The entranced person is probably always liable to mislead you; either through his view being at that time accidentally obscured; or through the influence of preconceived notions on his mind; or through the thoughts of others who are present influencing him. And an observer must always be on his guard against these unintentional sources of error, as well as against premeditated deception.

There are four principal applications to be made of these extraordinary powers, if they really exist.

I. To medical diagnosis and the treatment of disease.

II. To the solution of the higher philosophical problems.

III. To check irregular practices and even vicious thoughts; for you have only to consult the next somnambulist as to your neighbour's intentions, and he will tell you what they are.

IV. To the guidance of conduct, through learning what is in the womb of time. For it is ascertained that the trance-prevision discloses no, so to speak, brute fate, or unavoidable necessity, but only what will happen if things remain as they are; knowing which you may occasionally avert or avoid what is coming, by pursuing an altered course.

Now let us suppose the odds to be millions to one against all this being true, would it not still be worth while putting one'sself to considerable trouble for the merest chance of finding in the end such important results attainable? But the odds are less; for the genuineness of such details as I have given in the preceding pages is attested by a host of writers otherwise of unquestioned fidelity. And the trouble is little; for the outside of it is to go to Paris for a fortnight; or to pay M. Alexis for coming to London. The investigation itself would require some good sense, and much candor, and a full attention to all the reasonable precautions, which you would be told are necessary not to spoil at each sitting the state of trance.

CPSIA information can be obtained at www.ICGtesting.com
Printed in the USA
BVOW04s1439210316

441154BV00005B/50/P